Vital Breath of the Dao

Chinese Shamanic Tiger Qigong

Laohu Gong

Master Zhongxian Wu

海内存知己，天涯若比邻

史贤

Praise for Master Zhongxian Wu's
Vital Breath of the Dao

"In this beautiful book, Master Zhongxian Wu communicates to us his great understanding of, and experience with *Qigong*—not as a mere technique but as a perspective on life itself. He presents this material in a timeless way that engenders open awareness and ease of being in the reader. Over a cup of tea, we are led to taste the fruits of the practice so reverently offered to us. Master Wu is generous to create an elaborate context through the language of Classical Chinese Medicine as an initiation for us into the heart of teachings that too often remain hidden from the student. I recommend this book to all practitioners who have a serious interest in the deeper traditions of Chinese Medicine."

—**LONNY S. JARRETT**, author of *Nourishing Destiny* and *The Clinical Practice of Chinese Medicine*

"This book delivers the authentic teaching of shamanic *Qigong* and at the same time provides the cultural context that gave it birth. This sort of knowledge and understanding is rare nowadays, even among Chinese masters. How fortunate we are to have this first encyclopedic volume from Master Wu Zhongxian, which he shares with us as the old friends we are on this oldest of paths."

—**RED PINE (BILL PORTER)**, author of *The Road to Heaven*

"This book, in addition to practice instructions and novel *Qigong* techniques, provides a fascinating glimpse into the correlative and symbolic thinking of a traditionally trained *Qigong* master. Meandering creatively through linguistics and archaeology, myths and cosmic patterns, the author links *Qigong* practice with a kind of magico-synchronic thinking that is full of correspondences and sees matching coincidences on many levels of life. The book weaves a fabric rich in traditional stories, concepts, and terms, applied in a variegated pattern to the complexities of modern life. Living in this world can be a fulfilling and enriching experience, offering much more than the mere physical well-being and focused concentration that is commonly associated with *Qigong*."

—**LIVIA KOHN**, Professor of Religion and East Asian Studies, Boston University, author of *Daoism and Chinese Culture* and *Early Chinese Mysticism*

"*Qigong* integrates posture, movement, mind, and breath. Within *Qigong* there is softness and fluidity, strength and power, and internal focus and outward opening. By publishing this text on Chinese Shamanic Tiger *Qigong*, Zhongxian Wu has performed a great service in deepening our knowledge of *Qigong*, offering both the form itself and his understanding of how to lead a harmonious *Qigong* life."

—**PETER DEADMAN**, author of *A Manual of Acupuncture* and founder of *Journal of Chinese Medicine*

"A remarkable blend of interesting scholarship, valuable healing practices, and a gateway into the deep authentic tradition of Chinese Shamanism and the internal martial arts. It would take the journey of a lifetime in China to find such teachings and sincerity."

—**MICHAEL MAYER**, Ph.D. licensed Psychologist, *Qigong* teacher and author of *Secrets to Living Younger Longer: The Self-Healing Path of Qigong Standing Meditation and Tai Chi*

"This energetic English-language presentation of the worldview that informs the theory and practice of Shamanic *Qigong* is practical, easy to follow, and astonishingly comprehensive. Master Wu's lucid contemporary prose provides a valid passport to China's central province of healing: the appropriate regulation and deployment of the body. He talks to the reader as if to a friend across a table at a tea house, and he knows that if we each will only allow ourselves to accept the healing warmth he has poured out for us, the spirit of immediate living will fill our cup. We would be cranky to refuse."

—**JOHN BEEBE**, Jungian analyst, author of *Integrity in Depth*

"This is a remarkably interesting book by a remarkable master of many Chinese arts. Ostensibly about *Qigong*, this book penetrates deep into the roots of China's ancient shamanism. This alone makes it worthwhile reading, even for those who don't want to learn his powerful Shamanic Tiger *Qigong*. It is easily accessible even as it explains the complex original meanings of symbols and reveals the *Qigong* way of thinking, feeling, and moving through life. It explores the art of drinking tea, the I Ching, Taoist numerology and cosmology, and much more. Usually, I tell people to avoid books on *Qigong*, as you cannot learn the art from them. This book is the exception—don't miss it."

—**MICHAEL WINN**, founder, Healing Tao University, past president, National *Qigong* Association (NQA)

"Master Wu's sixth book—his first in English—is a seminal work in the field of *Qigong*. For Westerners interested in this fascinating healing art, it opens a window into the little-known Shamanic roots of *Qigong*. Master Wu's compassionate heart and sincere spirit offers readers a trusted guide through the cultural history of Chinese Shamanic *Qigong* and the practice of personal cultivation."
—**FRANCESCO GARRI GARRIPOLI**, author of *Qigong: Essence of the Healing Dance*

"This lovely book explores the symbolism, numerology, and theory of Chinese Shamanic *Qigong* in a way that will expand the horizons of both *Qigong* beginners and long-time practitioners alike. Zhongxian Wu invites us to drink tea with him while he tells us instructive stories about his own personal journey, all the time reminding us that there is 'no hurry,' and that only by slowing down, sensing, feeling, and breathing can we experience the essence of *Qigong*."
—**DENNIS LEWIS**, author of *The Tao of Natural Breathing* and *Free Your Breath, Free Your Life*

"Master Zhongxian Wu has given us a deeply illuminating perspective on the ancient Chinese Shamanic roots of *Qigong*. Masterfully described in this book, the wisdom tradition of Chinese shamanism is the source code of all classical Daoist and Confucian cultures. Wu teaches us that the original purpose of *Qigong* was to model a harmonious way of life by connecting with universal energy while simultaneously pointing to the possibility of spiritual cultivation. Master Wu has ably integrated a biographical, scholarly, and practical understanding of this tradition through story and myth, a deep knowledge of Shamanic symbolism, and his generous sharing of Shamanic *Qigong* techniques."
—**GUNTHER M. WEIL**, Ph.D.

"This is not a narrow book about a little known style of *Qigong*. Master Wu carefully and thoroughly explains the history and context out of which the Tiger *Qigong* style emerged. This book is the work of a true scholar, rich in detail yet presented in a very relaxed, easy-to-understand format. I recommend it to anyone who wants an in-depth look at the history and evolution of Chinese Shamanic *Qigong*."
—**MARK JOHNSON**, a founding father of the National *Qigong* Association (NQA)

"Master Wu has done a wonderful job in bridging the ancient world of Chinese Shamanism with the ongoing and ever unfolding world of Daoism. By explaining and clarifying the characters used in the traditional teachings he is able to convey a deeper understanding of these life-changing practices."
—**SOLALA TOWLER**, editor *The Empty Vessel*, author of *Tales From the Tao*

Vital Breath of the Dao
Chinese Shamanic Tiger Qigong
Laohu Gong

Master Zhongxian Wu

Substantive editing: Pamela Causgrove

Published in the United States by:
Dragon Door Publications, Inc
P.O. Box 4381, St. Paul, MN 55104
Tel: (651) 487-2180 • Fax: (651) 487-3954
Credit card orders: 1-800-899-5111
Email: dragondoor@aol.com • Website: www.dragondoor.com

ISBN   0-938045-68-7

Photography: Don Pitlik

Book design and cover by Derek Brigham
Website http//www.dbrigham.com
Tel/Fax: (612) 827-3431 • Email: dbrigham@visi.com

Manufactured in the United States
First edition: February 2006

DISCLAIMER

This book is for reference and informational purposes only and is in no way intended as medical counseling or medical advice. The information contained herein should not be used to treat, diagnose or prevent any disease or medical condition without the advice of a competent medical professional. The activities, physical or other-wise, described herein for informational purposes, may be too strenuous or dangerous for some people and the reader should consult a physician before engaging in them. The author and Dragon Door Publications shall have neither liability nor responsibility to any person or entity with respect to any loss, damage, or injury caused or alleged to be caused directly or indirectly by the information contained in this book.

Dedication

This book is dedicated to:

Tian 天 — *Father Heaven*

Di 地 — *Mother Earth*

Jun 君 — *Ancient Chinese Shamans/Emperors*

Qin 親 — *Ancestors of Human Beings, my ancestors, and my parents*

Shi 師 — *Masters who passed down the classical wisdom traditions through the generations, including my Masters:*

Yu Wencai 于文才

Yang Rongji/Yongji 楊榮籍/永積

Pei Xirong 裴錫榮

Yuanzhao Fashi 圓照灋師

Lama Dunzhu 喇嘛敦珠

Li Mingzhong 李明忠

Wang Jiayou 王家祐

Zhao Shourong 趙守榮

夏黍瓴

Acknowledgements

The universe weaves everything together in an invisible web according to its laws. I understood this at a deeper level by the time I had finished this book. It is partly the result of my hard work, but more than this, it is the fruit of the universal weaving *Qi*. This book would never have come to you without all of the support I have been given over a long time period—my personal time river.

Confucius said "Time passing is the same as the flowing water in the river." Past, present, and future are one, without separation and flowing like a river. A wisdom tradition is the baby of time. It needs nurturing in the time river; otherwise, the baby would easily die. Much ancient knowledge has perished through the passage of time. It is a blessing that the ancient knowledge we discuss in this book is still alive. From the bottom of my heart, I want to express my gratitude to those who have supported me in making and taking care of this new baby—*Vital Breath of the Dao*—in my past, present, and future:

Past The education and training from the past—my teachers and parents are the source of my writing. There are no words through which I can express my gratitude to them. I hold their spirits in my heart as my spiritual genetic code. With these spirits, I will do my best to pass down their knowledge and wisdom to my students and to serve others.

Present The help in the present—families, friends, publisher, editor, designer, students, and the Universal *Qi* are the reason this book became real. I want to acknowledge:

Pamela Causgrove for her contribution of countless hours to edit this book. This book would have taken much longer to arrive without her professional and continual editing during my writing process.

John Du Cane and his Dragon Door Publications for the support in bringing this book to us.

Derek Brigham for his creative design of this book.

Chungliang Al Huang, Bill Porter, Mark Johnson, Lonny Jarrett, Dennis Lewis, Livia Kohn, Michael Winn, Francesco Garri Garripoli, John Beebe, Michael Mayer, Gunther Weil, Peter Deadman, and Solala Towler for their reviews of my book and helpful suggestions.

Tom Pasley, David Branscomb, Joanne Wu, Katherine Delleney, Leonora Perron, Greg Wilson, Motoe Wada, Karen Fong, Daisy Lee Garripoli, and Sally Nissen for their suggestions and help in my teaching and writing.

Deirdre Orceyre for her loving support throughout the creation of this new baby.

Future The support in the future—you are the momentum to keep this book alive. I want to thank you for your willingness to read this book. Through pursuing a harmonious life, through seeking the roots of natural healing modalities, through spiritual cultivation, and through your quest for Enlightenment, you keep the ancient wisdom alive.

Zhongxian Wu

Foreword

by Chungliang Al Huang

Founder-President, Living Tao Foundation

Author, **Embrace Tiger, Return To Mountain: The Essence of Tai Ji**

I first met Wu Zhongxian through our mutual friend Red Pine, the eminent translator of Daoist and Zen Buddhist classics and Chinese poetry. When they came to visit me a few years ago during my Living Tao seminar at our River House in Gold Beach, Oregon, I was immediately impressed with the pureness and transparency of this young master. We became instant kindred friends, sharing in our Chinese heritage and many legacies. Wu was easily integrated into our circle of lifelong Dao friends, and graciously offered his learning/teaching, played his *Guqin*, and chanted *Tang* poetry with us as we practiced our *Tai Ji* moves.

I admire Master Wu's solid foundation of classical training in China and his innovative *Qigong* and *Tai Ji* teaching in the West. I have enjoyed reading several of his written contributions in a number of recent periodicals.

I am especially delighted to have the honor to review the manuscript of his book, *Vital Breath of the Dao*.

Master Wu has succeeded in introducing the Shamanic aspect of the ancient Daoist heritage, the first time ever so clearly in English. Through the magic of symbolic Chinese written metaphors and accessible, clear language, he has managed to explain these ancient ways to modern readers with clarity and ease.

It is indeed the talent of an enlightened teacher who is able to help Westerners in experiencing these seemingly much too exotic and esoteric teachings. I applaud Master Wu for this remarkable accomplishment.

Introduction

Vital Breath of the Dao—Chinese Shamanic Tiger Qigong will be the first English book about Chinese *Wu* 巫 (Shamanic) *Qigong*. This book is about the ancient Chinese wisdom tradition and its spiritual cultivation.

Wu 巫 —Chinese Shamanism—is the origin of Chinese civilization and culture. In the *Wu* 巫 perspective, the balance and union of Heavenly *Yang* and Earthly *Yin Qi* (energies) result in a peaceful and harmonious world. Likewise, imbalances in these energies can result in disharmony in the world, which can take the form of natural disasters such as earthquakes, storms, floods, and volcanic explosions. As part of this dynamic universe, human beings are also subject to the effects of these energies. By following and living by the balancing principles of the universe, it is possible to achieve harmony in the body. Through study and observation of this universal way, the ancient Chinese *Wu* (shamans or sages) created numerous methods to help people maintain/rebuild their body balancing systems in order to keep their physical bodies, minds, and spirits healthy. People have used these methods to improve their lives for thousands of years in China. Now, we call these modalities *Qigong*.

Qigong is a practice for cultivating inner knowledge and a way to help people return to the union of the Human Being and the Universe. *Qigong* facilitates the development of a deeper relationship with *Qi*, which helps the practitioner understand the laws of the universe and how they influence human life.

As a practitioner of some of the *Wu* traditions, I want to share my experience with westerners. The reason I am bringing the reader into my personal experience is that in the course of my *Wu* (Shamanic) *Qigong* practice, I have realized that the external world is a reflection of the heart and that a peaceful world is brought into existence by the whole of humanity. As a microcosm in the macrocosm, the physical body is a reflection of the heart as well. I hope that through sharing my story, this ancient wisdom will inspire more people to move into a state of well-being and bring peace to the world. In writing *Qigong* books and articles, my intent is not to teach techniques, but to share the way of my life, the experience of my *Qigong* practice, and the ancient wisdom I am cultivating.

In ancient times, the *Wu* used the ancient Chinese characters as a vehicle to access the universal *Qi* and circulate the energy network. One of the unique features of this book is that I use Chinese characters to share this knowledge.

This book is comprised of three parts. In Part I, I describe my experience of life as a way of sharing my understanding of *Qigong*. I bring in some practical *Qigong* ideas and Chinese culture through the telling of my story. In Part II, I share some fundamental knowledge of Chinese Shamanic *Qigong*. This includes symbolism, numerology, and theory. In Part III, I go into the details of the practice. In this part, I share the techniques from the ancient *Wu* and their cultural background, philosophy, and function.

Another unique feature of this book is that classical Chinese wisdom traditions are taught through joyous stories. It may give the reader a fresh view of *Qigong* even if he/she is an expert *Qigong* practitioner. This book will also be a good introduction for *Qigong* beginners. It can be a classical Chinese medical student textbook as well and is a relaxing read for people who are interested in Classical Chinese culture and anthropology.

Live in harmonious *Qi*!

Zhongxian Wu

Table of Contents

Vital Breath of the Dao —
Chinese Shamanic Tiger Qigong
Laohu Gong 老虎功

Part II *Han San He Yi* 含三合一
— **Holding Three in One**
The Fundamentals of Chinese Shamanic *Qigong*

Part III *Laohu Gong* 老虎功
— Chinese Shamanic Tiger *Qigong* Form

PART I

Pin Ming Lun Dao

品茗論道

Tea and the Dao

The Dao is subtle; to understand it is to taste that which cannot be tasted.[1]

道之出口　淡乎其無味

Dao Zhi Chu Kou
Dan Hu Qi Wu Wei

Τhis book is about the classical Chinese wisdom tradition of *Qigong*. *Qigong* is a way of physical and spiritual cultivation, and it is also a way of life. Through understanding our lives, we can improve our spiritual cultivation. For this reason, I want to share a little of my life experience with you as an introduction to *Qigong* practice. Tea is an important part of my life. I learned the natural way of life, the teachings of the ancient Chinese shamans, and my spiritual path through drinking tea. In this first part of the book, I would like to share the tea experience with you. Hold on a minute. Please make a cup of tea for yourself first.

道灋自然

Dao Fa Zi Ran

The Dao Models Itself on the Way of Nature

1.1 *Man* 慢 (Slow Down) — The Way of Life

What is your feeling? Does your hot tea slow down our conversation? Yes? Great! This is the important experience. In Chinese, we can use the character *Man* 慢 to stand for this way of life. *Man* 慢 is composed of the left radical for heart and the right radical for graceful and prolonged. It is an image of a person taking a long time to enjoy a graceful life with the heart. Please enjoy your tea with your heart. Now I want to start my story about my experience with American life.

1.1.1 Go Slowly

Life here in America is much different from the life I had in China. My first feeling about life in American culture is that life is a rush. In China, the traditional way of life is called *Man* 慢, which means that everything should slow down. *Man* is a way of meditation, and it is also the way of a natural lifestyle. In Chinese, *Man* carries more meanings than its literal translation into English as "slow." It includes the experience of relaxing, enjoying oneself, and—through an intentional, or mindful, leisureliness—remaining calm in all actions and in all situations. This is the essential experience gained over thousands of years by ancient Chinese people living a natural lifestyle. Now, modern China is being widely affected by western culture and daily life is getting more and more rushed.

Traditionally in China, when we start to eat, we say "*Manchi* 慢吃"—Eat slowly—in the same way the French say, "*Bon appétit.*" And instead of saying goodbye in China, we say, "*Manzou* 慢走"—Go slowly. Although I am living in a continually modernizing world, I want to maintain the attitude of enjoying my life; therefore, I often remind myself of my ancient ancestors' wisdom: *Man*, slow down, no rush, enjoy the moment. Especially in my *Qigong* practice, the first important thing to do is this: *Man*, slow down.

1.1.2 Time Schedule and the Car

One of the major differences I have noticed between Chinese and American lifestyles is the way time is handled. When I first came here, it was a big shock to see that everyone had a schedule book. As I started working with people in the U.S., I found that everything had to be planned ahead. I felt that I could not enjoy the moment when I tried doing this. I had to think about what I would be doing in the next hour, even in the next minute. It seemed to me that one day's life was not whole. It was divided into many small pieces. I have tried not to make too many plans in a day, and I have never used a schedule book in all my time here. I am trying to maintain my daily life in oneness.

Another difference I have noticed is in the way people use transportation. Most people in China don't have cars. In fact, I didn't know how to drive until I came here. In the U.S., most people rely on the car, and now so do I. It's like some friends told me, "Life here without a car is the same as a person without legs." I don't mean that a car is not good in our lives. I realize that a car brings convenience to my life. However, nothing in our world is entirely good or bad. According to ancient Chinese *Yin-Yang* philosophy (See Part II, 5.3 *Liangyi* 兩儀 — *Yin Yang*), there should be a *Yang* aspect if there is a *Yin* aspect. The car is a symbol for high speed. To accomplish the daily tasks of our lives, we have to use a car because it can help us speed up our lives. Unfortunately, most of us aren't aware that this kind of speed makes the mind go crazy. As *Laozi* tells us, "An excess of hunting and chasing makes your mind go crazy."[2] Slow is a safe way of life. For instance, when we are driving during rush hour, we may cause an accident if we hurry and drive too fast. Sometimes when I drive on the freeway, I tell myself to slow down my breath and allow my consciousness and my mind to stay calm. Otherwise, my mind may go "crazy."

1.1.3 Take Your Time

This is the picture I get from American life. In fact, we waste much time in the car on the way to different places when daily life is sectioned into increments of time. When I worked eight hours a day as an engineer in China, I didn't feel rushed or stressed because I stayed in one place—no car, no going out for anything, no leaving for appointments. Everything was there. During break times, I could drink my tea (I had a tea set in my office) and read a book. I had time to practice my *Qigong* and martial arts, play my music, and write my *Qigong* books after work. I could enjoy myself without rushing. When the physical body is more settled down, the heart/mind will be more settled down.

Another difference I've noticed here in the U.S. is that there are so many short seminars offered. Taking a seminar is a good way to learn some new techniques in such a rushed society. In China, although people's lives are getting rushed and modernized, there are not so many short seminars. The reason, I think, is that the root of traditional Chinese culture may still be deeply affecting modern China.

Qigong, Taijiquan, martial arts, Chinese medicine, and the other classical Chinese wisdom traditions may all look like techniques, but they are not merely techniques. They are types of culture, philosophy, meditation, and knowledge that can be gained only through experience and practice over a long period of time. In China, training is more grounded. We need to *"Hua Gongfu"* (take our time), as we say in Chinese. I have followed masters for many years, maybe my entire life, in different classical Chinese arts training and practice. In my *Qigong*, martial arts, Chinese astrology, music, and calligraphy practice, I remember that all of my masters told me, "No rush. Slow down. Take your time."

I have spent four years in the U.S. and have published a number of papers in journals on *Qigong*, martial arts, and oriental medicine to explain what *Qigong* is, how it benefits our lives, and where it comes from. Although I have received some good feedback on these articles from publishers and *Qigong* practitioners, I still have a feeling that there is more for me to do. I feel I should continue achieving my life mission to live *Qigong* and to spread *Qigong* by writing my books. I understand it will take time to finish this work.

1.2 *Cha* 茶 (Tea) — The Way of Spiritual Cultivation

Now I invite you to read and experience my *Qigong* life. Please send your spiritual body with me. Don't know how? It is not difficult. One of the key elements of *Qigong* practice is visualization. Please do not hurry. This is the way of *Qigong*, no hurry. Perhaps it will take me a while to tell you about *Qigong*.

Imagine that you and I are together in a teahouse in a natural setting. It is a very simple house built of logs. We are sitting at the tea table, and we can see flowers and grass outside and a living stream running in front of the house. We can see the forest through the side windows. We can hear birds singing in the sunshine. Now please stop reading and close your eyes. Take some time to imagine this. Feel the relaxation, peace, and harmony in your inner world.

1.2.1 *Gongfu* and Tea

Thank you for trying the visualization. Allow me to make some tea for us—*Gongfu* 功夫 tea. This tea is similar to my lifestyle. You may be curious about *Gongfu* Tea and wonder what it is. It is a style of drinking tea and a tea ceremony. It requires *Hua Gongfu* (taking time) to prepare and drink this tea. In Chinese, *Gongfu* means time. It also means a skill that develops over a long time and through strenuous effort. This implies rigorous repetition of drills, both verbal and physical. *Gongfu* also means martial arts. Chinese country folk say "*Gongfu*" rather than "martial arts." In modern China, people still widely use the term "*Gongfu*" to evaluate a person's skill and talent in a particular line of work. "No *Gongfu*" means to be without skill or to do a poor job.

Are you ready for a cup of tea? There are two small cups facing you on the tea table. One is a cylinder and the other one is a bowl. After washing and warming up the tea set with boiling water, I make the tea for our tea ceremony using the Jade Red Phoenix Oolong that I brought back from China. I am filling up your cylinder cup with the hot Oolong. Please cover it with the bowl cup for a minute. Be careful, it is hot. Now you can hold the cylinder cup with your middle finger and index finger, and the bowl cup with your thumb. Hold it above the tea table and turn it over. Pretty good job! You leaked only a little bit of tea from your cups onto the table.

Are you ready for the tea? Please take a deep breath, then breathe out and imagine releasing all the old air *(Qi)* from your body. Empty the body and hold—hold your breath, hold the empty state. Next, hold the cylinder and raise it gently, allowing the tea to flow into the bowl cup. Put the mouth of the empty cylinder cup right under your nose. Now take a deep breath from the cup to absorb all the air down into your lower belly. Did you enjoy it? Yes, it is an enjoyable and relaxing experience.

1.2.2 Wordlessness

Tell me, what are you feeling? Difficult to say? No words can express your feeling? Yes, that's your experience. Language always fails to totally express the feeling. Confucius said, "Writing does not fully express words, and words do not fully express ideas."[3] It is the same with *Qigong* practice—you can experience it only when you do it yourself in the right way. *Laozi* explains this process in Chapter 2 of the *Daodejing* 道德經:

聖人處無為之事	*The Sage relies on actionless activity,*
行不言之教	*Carries on wordless teaching,*
萬物作焉而不辭	*Lets all things rise and fall,*
生而不有	*Nurtures, but does not interfere,*
為而不恃	*Acts without demanding,*
功成而不居	*Accomplishes, but claims no credit,*
夫惟弗居	*It is because he lays claim to no credit*
是以不去	*That the credit cannot be taken away from him.*

At last you can drink your tea. It's a small cup of tea, but don't swallow it all at once or it will hurt you. It is hot! Sip a little with your lips softly touching the edge of the cup. Hold it in your mouth. Taste it with the tip of your tongue and the coat of your tongue. Then swallow it slowly, feeling it pass through your throat and down into your *Dantian* 丹田.[4] This process is called *Pin* 品 in Chinese. The literal English translation of *Pin* is taste or savor, but this does not convey its deeper meaning. *Pin* is also the way of study and meditation in classical Chinese culture. This is a way of classical Chinese spiritual cultivation, which we call *Chadao* 茶道 (the Dao of tea). One may become enlightened by drinking tea.

Chinese characters are originally and basically pictorial characters, so they have symbolic meanings embedded within them. Through the *Pin*, one can enter deeply into the classical Chinese way of life, way of thinking, and cultural background. Let's learn more about the Chinese characters to help us better understand them.

1.3 *Wen* 文 (Pattern) — The Way of the Universe

Let us continue to enjoy our tea and discuss the function of the Chinese characters. We call this way of learning *Pin Ming Lun Dao* 品茗論道. It means to discuss and understand the Dao through the taste of the tea. This is the lifestyle of the classical Chinese sages and scholars. We can adopt this style and continue to discover the way to connect with the Dao.

1.3.1 The Chinese Character and its Origin

Chinese characters make up the last ancient ideographic or pictographic writing system that survives in modern usage. This unbroken system has been continued for thousands of years. It is possible to learn the ancient Chinese wisdom through the symbolic meanings of the characters. The original function of the Chinese characters was not merely to serve as a means of communication; rather, the characters were intended to serve as a vehicle for channeling universal wisdom and for connecting with nature. Below are two creation stories about Chinese characters connected with *Wu* 巫 (Chinese shamanism) that demonstrate this function.

The *Han* Dynasty (140 BCE–220 CE) Chinese dictionary *Shouwen Jiezi* states that *Cangjie* 仓頡 , who was a minister of *Huangdi* 黃帝 (the Yellow Emperor) about 4,500 years ago, formed the Chinese characters after observing patterns of animal tracks and combining them with trigrams.[5] This legend also tells us that at the moment *Cangjie* created these characters, it was storming heavily and the spirits were weeping[6]—reminiscent of the *Wu* (shaman) calling in the rains. The spirits' weeping in the story reminds us that these characters affected those spirits. In my *Wu* practice, I use some Chinese characters as special symbols to channel the universal energy to empower my body and align my spiritual energy or to help patients release disease.

Archeological research indicates that possible precursors to Chinese characters appeared as early as 8,000 years ago. However, unearthed inscriptions on bone and tortoise shell show that a complete system of Chinese character writing had been in use during the *Shang* 商 Dynasty (1700–1027 BCE). Since these inscriptions were related to the divination practices of the *Shang* emperors, this style of character is called *Jiaguwen* 甲骨文 Oracle Script. For this reason, we can see that the Chinese characters were invented by ancient shamans and that *Cangjie* was one of them.

Chinese character inscribed on a turtle shell discovered in *Henan* Province; from about 8,000 years ago.

A copy of calligraphy from a *Zhou* Dynasty (1027 to 221 BCE) stone carving.

1.3.2 *Wen* 文 (Pattern) and *Wu* 巫 (Shaman)

We can find more stories about the relationship between the Chinese characters and *Wu*. The Chinese character *Wen* 文, meaning Chinese character, may give us more information. Let's have another cup of tea and talk about the Chinese character *Wen* 文.

The original meaning of *Wen* is natural pattern. This pattern could be made up of cracks, tracks, animal footprints, or clouds. It was said that *Wen* came from *Wu* ritual. During a divination process, the *Wu* would burn a scapula bone or tortoise shell. The bone or shell would break during burning and a pattern of cracks would appear. The shaman could get an answer to the question posed in the divination through the pattern of cracks. It was thought that the pattern was a symbol or character from Heaven or from a high-level spirit, and the ancient shamans applied these crack patterns to the ancient Chinese characters. For instance, the Chinese character for divination or to divine is *Bu* 卜. *Bu* looks like a pattern of cracks. The pronunciation of *Bu* is related to divination as well. The moment that the *Wu* was burning the bone or shell and the fire made the crack in the bone or shell, it made a noise—*Bu*. Therefore, the moment the shaman heard the sound of *Bu* the pattern was revealed and the answer for the divination became known.

This Oracle Script is still relevant today, especially the Seal Script or *Zhuan Shu* 篆書. The symbolic meaning of "*Zhuan* 篆 " is "to communicate with the universe through writing." It is related to the *Wu* book, the *Yijing* 易經 (Book of Changes or *I Ching*). The bottom radical of the character *Zhuan* is *Tuan* 彖, meaning boar, and it stands for the Big Dipper. In the *Yijing*, one of the rhetorical structures for explaining the meaning of each hexagram is to begin each line of the hexagram with "*Tuan Yue* 彖曰 "—Boar says or Big Dipper indicates. The radical on top of *Zhuan* is *Zhu* 竹, meaning bamboo. It is a hint that the Heavenly knowledge was originally recorded on bamboo. (Paper had not yet been invented.)

Ancient books written in Oracle or Seal Script were titled "*Tian Shu* 天書" (Heavenly Book) because people in ancient China trusted that the knowledge was channeled from Heaven through the shaman/sage. Even though the Chinese characters later changed to the Earthly way—square, the ancient Chinese always believed that the knowledge was from Heaven. Confucius said, "I record only the ancient knowledge without adding my own ideas [when I edit the old classics]. I always trust, respect, and love the ancient knowledge."[7] The *Han* Dynasty's *Sima Qian* 司馬遷, author of the *Shiji* 史記 (Book of History), referred to this way of thinking as "the Sage's attitude."[8] Its importance has not diminished over time, and this reverence for the ancient knowledge continues to be passed down. I remember my masters always told me as they taught me the ancient knowledge, "Do not make any changes in your practice; the right way is to follow the classical forms. This is what I learned from my master." This is how the ancient wisdom has been passed down. Through studying ancient Chinese characters, I understood my masters better and I have been following in their footsteps in teaching my students.

1.3.3 The Chinese Character and its Function

The tea is still strong. Let us continue drinking tea and talking about the Chinese characters. They carry so much information.

This Oracle Script is still relevant today, especially the Seal Script or *Zhuan Shu* 篆書 . *Zhuan Shu* includes *Xiao Zhuan* 小篆 (lesser seal character) and *Da Zhuan* 大篆 (greater seal character). *Xiao Zhuan* is the result of the power of the first emperor of the *Qin* 秦 Dynasty (221–206 BCE), *Qinshihuang* 秦始皇 . He asked his prime minister, *Lisi* 李斯 , to standardize the Chinese characters. By the way, did you watch the movie *Hero*? Yes, as you may have noticed in the movie, there were different writing styles for the same Chinese characters in different states before the *Qin* Dynasty. Through the principles of Oracle Script and ancient Chinese characters that had been cast in vessels or carved in rock, *Lisi* created the standardized Chinese character system for the whole nation. Later, people named this standardized system *Xiao Zhuan* and called all the older scripts *Da Zhuan*.

Seal Script is now used only in artistic seals or artwork. Although Seal Script carving and calligraphy remain art forms in China today, most people are not able to read them. Yet it is common to use a signature seal instead of a written personal signature in modern China. However, people may use modern Chinese characters in their signature seals rather than the traditional Oracle Script. The verification function of the seal still remains. It originates from Chinese shamanism. Seal is *Yin* in Chinese. *Yin* means connect, verify, or response. It is a name for mudra (hand position) in *Wu* (shamanic) practice. *Yin* is also a way to verify that a person is practicing the *Wu* tradition for communicating with spirits.

A copy of calligraphy; from a *Han* Dynasty stone carving

This type of writing hints at knowledge of the *Wu* cosmos. Most strokes in the Seal Script are rounded and the shape of the characters is circular. It is said that the *Han* Dynasty's *Chenmiao*

程邈 developed the Clerk Script (*Lishu* 隸書) for convenience. The strokes of Clerk Script are straight, and the pattern of the characters is square. This was the original model for the modern-day Chinese characters. Clerk Script is still easy to read. According to ancient Chinese cosmology, *"Tian Dao Yue Yuan Di Dao Yue Fang* 天道曰圓 地道曰方"* —Heaven is circular and Earth is square.[9] This cosmology became the basic Chinese philosophy. Therefore, in Chinese tradition, the circle is a symbol for Heaven and the square is a symbol for Earth. This philosophy is the fundamental principle of *Qigong, Taiji*, and other martial arts.

By now, it must be obvious to you that the Chinese character is a portal into deeper layers. So, what exactly is the function of the Chinese character? In Chinese, it is *WenYi Zai Dao* 文以載道. This means the function of a character is to carry the Dao, or to express and convey the Dao to people. *Qigong* is also a way to access the Dao. The difference is that *Qigong* is the experiential way and the Chinese character is the symbolic way. We are able to merge into the Dao through correct *Qigong* practice and can better understand the symbolic meaning. Turning this around, we can find a better way to practice *Qigong* through the symbolic meaning. Therefore, I use some Chinese characters in this book to help us better access the *Qigong* practice.

1.4 *Kou* 口 (Entrance) —The Way of Teaching

After we learn some more about the Chinese character, let's have another cup of tea. How about continuing our chat about Chinese characters with part of the Chinese character *Pin* 品? Why only part of *Pin* 品 rather than the whole character? Because we *Pin* (taste or savor) the tea and the Chinese characters with a part of *Pin* – *Kou* 口 (mouth). Also, it is the same way we drink the hot tea. We must take small sips, otherwise it may hurt us. Of course, the Chinese character will never hurt us physically, but I don't want us to feel overwhelmed or to misunderstand this due to our attitude of being in a hurry. Let us taste the Chinese characters as *Pin* 品 itself.

1.4.1 The Way of Subtlety

Pin is made up of three of the same radical—*Kou* 口 , which means mouth. There are two layers of symbolic meaning in these three radicals. The first one is three and the second one is mouth. Three means numerous; it does not mean simply the number three. Also, three means the three layers of the universe— Heaven, Earth, and the Human Being. Three is the creation number and it is the symbol for everything and the universe. Therefore, in classical Chinese, three stands for many or numerous. We will learn more about three in Part II of this book (See Part II, 5.4 *Sancai* 三 才/3—Three Sources). In this section, let us focus on the second meaning; it is also *Kou*.

Another cup of *Gongfu* 功夫 tea may help us better learn about this because we need to use our *Kou* (mouth) to experience the *Pin*.

You did a good job just now. No tea leaked when you turned over your cups. Repetition can make the experience different each time, and it will make you more skillful, too. We will have a similar experience as we practice *Qigong*. Can you tell the difference in the flavor of the tea? Yes, it is fantastic. It has a better taste compared with the first cup. How could this happen when this cup of tea comes from the same teapot as the first cup? We haven't changed the tea leaves, yet you can tell the difference with your *Kou*. This is the Universal Way. The Yellow Emperor called this *Jiwei Zi Dao* 幾微之道—the way of subtlety. We can understand the Dao 道 through careful observation. The Dao is in the tea. We can access it only through *Pin*.

1.4.2 The Entrance to the Dao

Kou 口 , again, means mouth. The second symbolic meaning of *Pin* is entrance. It is a symbol that represents human beings as well. The mouth is a very important entrance into the body because to stay alive we need to take food into our bodies every day through the mouth. In the Chinese medicine perspective, the mouth is connected with the heart/mind. When we speak, we open the mouth. Language is the voice of the heart. This is the original meaning in Chinese. We use our mouths to express what we are thinking, what we need, and what we want to communicate to others. The *Shuowen Jiezi* explains *"Kou* (mouth) —a person uses the mouth to speak and to eat." Moreover, the *Guoyu* 国语 (Conversations from the States) tells us that *"Kou* is the gate of the Three and the Five." Here, the Five is also the symbol of the universe. From ancient Chinese cosmology, the three layers of the universe are made from the Five Elements: Water, Wood, Fire, Earth, and Metal (See Part II, 5.6 *Wuxing* 五行 /5 — Five Elements). Therefore, we can learn how to connect our heart/spirit with the universe through the *Kou*.

Kou is the entrance to the Dao. The traditional way of *Qigong* teaching is "mouth to mouth." *Qigong* is the way of experiential knowledge. We could not learn *Qigong* by merely reading a book or watching a videotape. We can get the subtle feeling only by following a master in person. The traditional way in China for this kind of knowledge teaching is *"Kouchuan Xinshou* 口傳心授"— Teaching through the mouth and giving through the heart. This means that if we want to learn authentic *Qigong*, we must follow a true master. A book or video tape is only a way to help us remember what we have learned in the traditional Chinese way.

1.4.3 Root and Tip

It may seem easy for a beginner to grasp the superficial aspects of *Qigong* practice—or to get some physical exercise—through a book or video. However, it is possible that without personal guidance from a master, this approach may bring more harm than benefit. From the traditional perspective, this is the reverse way of learning. In Chinese, this perspective is called *"Ben Mo Dao Zhi—* 本末倒置." *Ben* 本 means a tree root, and *Mo* 末 means the tree tips. Let's look carefully at these two characters. *Ben* 本 will become Mo 末 if we raise the lower horizontal radical (bar) from *Ben*. The root becomes the tip! In contrast, *Mo* will become *Ben* (the tip becomes the root) if we lower the upper horizontal radical. However, we may regard the tip as the root if we are not learning *Qigong* correctly.

The Universal Way is subtle. The way of teaching should be from mouth to mouth—a student should learn from a master directly. The *Guiguzi* 鬼谷子

explains that "the mouth is the gate of the Heart." Experiential knowledge can be truly understood only by following the right way with a true master. Thus, *Kou* carries the symbolic meaning of being the entrance to traditional wisdom. This is the entrance to the Dao.

1.5 *Pin* 品 (Savor)—The Way of Study

After learning the meaning of *Kou* (mouth), we can now enter the mystical storage of *Pin* through the portal of tea. The Chinese character *Pin* has different layers of meaning, and it can be used as either a noun or a verb.

1.5.1 The Meaning of Three Mouths

First of all, as we know, three means many and *Kou* (mouth) means people. Accordingly, the original meaning of *Pin* is many people. One common meaning of the *Pin* is savor. We can thoroughly enjoy our life through the mouth. We can take in delicious foods and drinks to nourish our bodies with our mouths. We can sing sweet songs to satisfy our feelings with our mouths. We can communicate with our friends with our mouths.

Traditionally, Chinese people spend much time over their food. In modern times, people still like to spend half a day with friends or family at the dining table. This is a way of *Pin*—relaxed and cheerful—in our life. I am pleased to tell you that I spent at least 5 hours every day in restaurants with my friends during my visit to China this past summer (2004). The first thing I did upon meeting my friends was to get food. Can you believe it? In Chinese tradition, can you guess what the first words we use to greet each other are? We say, "Have you eaten?" We will understand the symbolic meaning of *Pin* by learning the traditional Chinese ideas about food.

1.5.2 The Dao of Food

Food is one of the most important factors in our lives. Ancient Chinese sages devoted enormous amounts of research to food and had fruitful results. In modern times, we consider the nutritional value of the food we eat. What is the best nutrition for my body? Does this food have the nutritional content that my doctor recommends? Yet during ancient times in the classical Chinese way, people thought about their food as more than simply material or fuel for the body; they thought about food quality in the energetic layer—*Qi*. Just as our tea quenches more than our thirst, food satisfies more than our hunger. Food is also a type of Chinese herbal medicine that contains different qualities of *Qi*. Moreover, different kinds of food have different kinds of *Qi*. Each type of food has its own particular shape, color, flavor, and smell. These characteristics are the expression of *Qi* and each characteristic belongs to one of the Five Elements. They connect with Universal *Qi* from different directions and with our body systems. A good doctor can help a patient recover from disease through the pattern of the food, through the color of the food, through the flavor of the food, and through the smell of the food. Food *Qi* can spread directly to the meridians and the organ system through *Kou*, the mouth.

At this moment, when we taste our tea, we are not only enjoying the flavor, but we can also feel it connect with our bodies and minds. We are learning a way to discover how the smells, flavors, and colors connect with the body and satisfy our physical and spiritual bodies. Therefore, we drink tea not only because we are thirsty; indeed, we drink tea to enjoy relaxation and harmony as we experience a natural way of life.

Now, let us explore more information on food. Some foods we enjoy very much in the regular way. This means the body needs this particular food because it really connects with us. If we don't like a particular food, then it is difficult to take it in, which means the energy may not be good for us. We may lose this natural protective function when we get sick. A good doctor can help us figure this out. The doctor may ask a patient to use some "bad" (distasteful to that person) food to revive the body's natural protective function.

How can food be transformed to be part of the body? In the Chinese way, a good dish should have three key elements: *Wei* 味 (flavor), *Xiang* 香 (odor), and

Se 色 (color). Through the mouth, we taste the flavor; through the nose, we smell the odor; through the eyes, we see the color. Ancient Chinese sages knew that these three key elements are associated with the body. From the perspective of Chinese shamanism, there are three key components in our body—*Jing* 精 (essence), *Qi* 气 (vital energy), and *Shen* 神 (spirit). *Jing* relates more to flavor; *Qi* more to odor; and *Shen* more to color. Thus, we use the flavor, odor, and color of food to nourish life.

1.5.3 Food as Herbal Medicine

In ancient Chinese herb documents, herbs are described in terms of flavor, odor, and color as well. The Chinese have a saying, "*Yao Si Tong Yuan* 藥食同源" —Medicine and food have the same source. Accordingly, we talk about what kind of flavor, what kind of odor, or what kind of color is good for each organ system in our *Qigong* practice. We may also discuss how flavor, odor, and color are beneficial to specific meridians or how they can help to release different kinds of disease.

For example, what kind of food is good for the Liver? Using a Chinese food and herb perspective, we will first think about the Liver system in terms of the Five Elements principle. Because the Liver is a Wood organ, it follows that everything related to the Wood element is beneficial to the Liver. This includes green color, sour flavor, and rancid odor. Thus, if someone has a disease related to the Liver, we can use green color to treat this condition. We can use sour flavor food, like vinegar, to treat liver disease. Also, food with a rancid odor can be used to treat this kind of patient.

I have a true story to tell you about using this approach to treat disease. A country Chinese medicine doctor used Chinese pickle juice (usually the odor is stinky and the flavor is sour) to treat a group of cancer patients and had good results. Now, do not simply copy this idea to work with your cancer patients. Again, I want to emphasize that in this book I am not teaching any techniques for treating patients but only sharing some ideas with you. You should follow an authentic classical Chinese medicine doctor if you want to learn healing techniques.

1.5.4 A Pathway to the Dao

If we want to understand more details of this food system, we need to comprehend the Five Elements principle (See Part II, 2.6 *Wuxing* 五行/5 — Five Elements). The *Pin* shows us the way human beings connect with the universe and with nature. Thus, we are not just thinking about satisfying our thirst or hunger when we are drinking or eating. Beyond this, we are experiencing a pathway to the Dao.

Ancient *Wuxing* or Five Element wheel made of bronze.

Now, we can more easily see the reason that another layer of meaning of *Pin* is related to appreciating life. When used as a verb, *Pin* also means to appreciate life. For example, if we love a book and take time to read it again and again, we call it *Pin Su* 品書—taste the book. The deeper layer of *Pin Su* is that your heart is in the book and you understand the Way.

Similarly, *Qigong* practice also needs *Pin*—careful repeating. After spending a few days learning a new form from my master, I always spent much more time to *Pin* it by myself (practice it again and again). By learning through this method, I understood a proverb from Chinese cultivation: "You will understand everything about the form after you repeat it ten thousand times."

Pin has many more meanings, such as equal, same level, class or classify, quality, or criticize. You can find a good Chinese dictionary, make a cup of tea, and take your time to *Pin* by yourself. This is the traditional Chinese way of study.

2

天網恢恢
Tian Wang Hui Hui

The Universal Network

I believe that you will figure out many more details of the Chinese character *Pin* and its symbolic connections. *Pin* is also the symbol for establish. *Pin* hints that you can see clearly the things that have been created. The *Yijing* (*I Ching* or Book of Changes) describes this meaning as "*Pin Wu Xian Zhang* 品物咸章 "—Everything had been clearly and obviously created already.[10] It also means that a thing can exist or have its internal factors connected with external factors. In the Chinese way, we say everything must have three factors in order to exist. We also say that there is a reason for creating things, and we call this *Yuanqi* 緣起. Now, let's get another cup of tea to talk about *Yuanqi*.

Yuanqi is also the classical Chinese style for the introduction to a book. But like all Chinese characters, it carries a much deeper meaning than this translation into English. I want to introduce these two Chinese characters to start talking about the motivation for writing my *Qigong* book in English.

2.1 *Yuan* 緣 (Edge) —The Karmic Relationship

The original meanings of *Yuan* 緣 include the edge of a vessel, a predestined relationship, depend on, reason, because, along, climb up, or the luck by which people are brought together.

2.1.1 Edges

Please drink another cup of tea and observe your action. Did you put the edge of the cup against your lips, the edge of your mouth? Yes! You could not really enjoy the tea if the two edges did not touch. You can feel the tea smoothly entering your mouth through the edge and *Pin* (taste) it.

The edge of a vessel, such as a teacup, enables us to bring nourishment into the body. As the edge of the cup is brought to our lips, it connects us with the tea and all the nourishment in the cup and it brings us into a state of oneness. Without the edge of the vessel, without the cup of tea, the nourishment could not connect with the body. In fact, no thing or event exists in isolation; each thing or event is connected with everything else, through both visible and intangible "edges." Ask yourself: Who am I? Why am I here? Why am I happy in one moment and unhappy in another moment? Why do I meet you at this time today rather than some other time? You may find the edges and get your answers through careful observation.

2.1.2 Inner Observation

To observe is the way of *Qigong*. When we practice, we need to observe our own bodies and understand what is happening. We need to understand how the energy is working in our bodies and connecting with the outside environment and the universe. Observing our daily lives, observing the outside world, and observing the connection is also the way of *Qigong*. The famous *Song* 宋 Dynasty scholar *Zhou Dunyi* 周敦颐 pointed this out in his poem: "You can understand the ten thousand things through quiet observation." Now, please drink your tea and continue your observations.

We can learn that the deepest layer of *Yuan* is karmic, or destined relationship, through our inner observation. When two people meet and become friends, it is because many conditions have created the relationship. If the connections are not there, then the relationship could not be formed because the two people would never meet. Think about it—Why am I having tea with you rather than someone else today? Are there not fifty billion people in this world? I came from the other side of the Pacific Ocean to meet you. Is it not amazing? Why did you pick up this book? Close your eyes and meditate on it. I believe that you will get the *Yuan* 緣—answer.

In Buddhist tradition, there's a teaching about this. The Buddha said two people could take the same boat across the river, thereby having a chance to meet. The real reason for their getting together, though, is that they did cultivation and practiced together for over 500 years and now they have the chance to meet in this lifetime in this boat. The deeper connections are there. Every day we do something or meet someone, and there is always a reason. It is not just coincidence. It's destiny, a type of karma and connection. This is a *Yuan*.

2.2 *Qi* 起 (Establish) — The Momentum of Existence

The original meaning of *Qi* 起 is the movement from lying down to sitting up and from sitting up to standing up. It also means produce, happen, start, origin, draw up, insurgence, help, sustain, construct, levy, employ, arouse, remove, open, carry, come from, group, case, or upward direction.

2.2.1 Do It

Let us use the example of building a house to learn the Chinese character *Qi* 起. All the materials have been gathered and are lying there on the ground, yet they cannot be made into a house without effort. A person has to make the effort to pick up the materials and work with them to construct the house. In the same way, if we are just lying down and want to do things, we must first have an intention, a purpose, or a goal. It is this that helps us achieve our purpose.

Without this, we can never do anything. To get started, we must first sit up, then stand up, and then start the process. Otherwise, we can accomplish nothing.

Qi 起 is the way of *Qigong* 气功. Yesterday, a new student took my *Qigong* class. I asked her, "Do you have any experience with *Qigong*?" She said, "Yes, I have some experience from a *Qigong* book." After the class, she excitedly told me, "It was a totally different experience from what I got from the book." Yes, *Qigong* is an experiential knowledge. We can understand it only through our bodies. It is like the tea. What is the feeling of drinking tea? I could not use my words to explain it because no words can explain it better than tasting it. Perhaps we have some good ideas about how to do something. However, nothing will happen if we only talk about it. Let us get up and do it. This is the *Qi* 起.

2.2.2 Do What You Say

In Confucianism, the process of *Zhi Xing He Yi* 知行合一 is the *Qi* 起 as well. *Zhi* 知 means understand or knowledge. *Xing* 行 means action, move or do. *He* 合 means combine. *Yi* 一 means one or together. When these words are combined, they mean that our actions should fit our hearts. In other words, it means we understand nothing if we have much knowledge but never use it. In our lives, we should do what we know and what we say we will do. This is the secret key to success.

An idea or knowledge is like a seed planted in the heart. We must have soil, water, and sunshine to make the seed grow. These factors are *Yuan* 緣 (edges). In addition, we need to take care of the seed. It needs the right nourishing environment, one that is conducive to growth. These conditions are *Qi* 起 (successful processes). Therefore, *Yuan* and *Qi* are the reason for the existence of everything. If there were only *Yuan* in the world or only *Qi* in the world, or neither *Yuan* nor *Qi* in the world, then there would be nothing but emptiness in the world.

2.3 *Kong* 空 (Emptiness) — The Universal Web

The two characters together, *Yuanqi* 緣起, also means the inherent reason events happen. For instance, I am writing this book because there is *Yuanqi* (reason and conditions, see Part I, 3 *Dong Xi Yuan Tong* 東西圓通 —The Pathway of *Yin Yang*). The conditions must be right to enable the action. Why do I build the teahouse or why do I start the project? Moreover, how can I start the project? Do I have all the help, knowledge, support and right timing, to make things happen? We can find the answers if we know emptiness through *Yuanqi*.

2.3.1 The Nature of Emptiness

The right conditions exist to help these things grow. It is the same as seeds needing the soil, water, sunshine, and other right conditions to help them grow. They need to connect with others. Otherwise, there would be no plants, flowers, or fruit. The world was created because all of the right conditions were present and connected. Nothing would exist if these conditions or connections were broken. Therefore, everything has the potential to be broken and this broken character we call *Kong* 空 (emptiness) in Chinese.

In shamanic tradition, a spider web represents the Universal Web

For example, we use the teacup to drink the tea. Now, I throw the teacup on the ground. What happens? It breaks and shatters into small pieces. Can we call these pieces a teacup and use them to drink tea? No! We call them "trash" and let them go to the trash can. The reason we cannot use the teacup anymore is that I have broken the conditions for its existence.

We will better understand emptiness in *Qigong* practice if we can understand more deeply the universal connection. The universe has a vast, invisible web connecting everything. Nothing can leak out from this web. This is what *Laozi* described as "*Tian Wan Hui Hui Shu Er Bu Lo* 天網恢恢 疏而不漏" —Heaven's web is vast with a big mesh weave, yet nothing slips through.[11]

2.3.2 The Oneness

According to ancient Chinese cosmology, the universe is one. The universe started from one mass of *Qi* 炁 . A different quality of *Qi* 炁 started moving in the primordial stage. The light *Qi* 炁 ascended to form Heaven and the heavy *Qi* 炁 descended to form Earth. Later, Heavenly *Qi* 炁 descended and Earthly *Qi* 炁 ascended, and then intercourse occurred between Heaven and Earth and gave birth to the ten thousand things (everything). The human being is the most treasured of the ten thousand things. Everything originated from the *Qi* 炁 and is connected together through the *Qi* 炁 . Three is the creation number, as we talked about before. Here, we can see that three is the symbol for universal creation. Please see Part II, 6.1 *Qi* 气 — Vital Energy for details of *Qi* 炁.

Let us have a new cup of tea and continue the tea drinking and read Part II, 4.2 *Shenhua* 神話 (Myth)—The Union of Humans and Spirits to enjoy a Chinese creation myth—the ancient story of *Pangu* 盤古. This creation story can help us better understand the universal web that interconnects the human being and the universe.

Did you learn something from the *Pangu* story? Yes, the universe has its own law, often referred to as the Way or the Dao, that weaves a web with *Qi* 炁. We are living in the web and belong to the web. Therefore, we should follow the Dao. My *Qigong* practice has made me more aware of the *Qi* 炁, more awake in my super-consciousness, and I have learned more about how the physical body and spiritual body connect with the universe through *Qi* cultivation. I can feel that my physical body, mental body, and spiritual body are well when my body *Qi* flows and connects with universal *Qi*. I have gotten sick when I have had *Qi* stagnation or have been disconnected from nature. As I recognized this connection, I understood that my body is not "mine," and I realized that the truth is "the Great Dao uses Emptiness as its real body."

In short, *Qigong* is a way to awaken the *Qi*, the universal web or network, the emptiness. *Qigong* is the way to maintain wellness in the web. As a tiny knot of the net, I know that my karmic mission is to live *Qigong* and spread *Qigong*. That's the reason I came from the East to the West. We can discuss more details of my story after another cup of tea.

東西圓通

Dong Xi Yuan Tong

The Pathway of Yin Yang

How is your tea? Too weak? Yes, it is too weak. But the tea will show its true flavor in the weak form. It is just like a relationship; time and space can measure how deeply you connect with another person. No matter how far away your friend is, no matter how many years have passed since you have seen your friend, true friends always keep deeply connecting in the spiritual layer. In Chinese, we say, "The relationship between Gentlemen (enlightened beings) is as thin as water." The flavor of the tea is fading, but fading is the way of the everlasting. *Laozi* explains this Universal Way as, "Fading implies far-reaching; far-reaching implies reversion to the original source."[12] This is similar to the way the sun disappears in the West and returns to the East the next morning. Actually, a traditional way to learn the *Yin-Yang* 陰陽 principle and the Dao is to observe the sun (*Yang*) and the moon (*Yin*). The moon is the reflection of the sun. Learning about the moon is a way to learn about the sun. When your back is to the North and your face is to the South, East is on your left and West is on your right. The sun rises from the East (left) and the moon begins its journey from the West (right). The sun is *Yang* and the moon is *Yin*. In Chinese tradition, therefore, left is *Yang* and right is *Yin*. The most important Chinese Medicine Classic, *Huangdi Neijing* 黄帝内經 (Yellow Emperor's Classic of Medicine), describes left-right as the pathway of *Yin-Yang*.[13]

Diagram for facing south during inner cultivation

In Chinese cosmology, the Chinese characters *Dong* 東 and *Xi* 西 not only stand for the directions East and West but also represent the seasons of spring and autumn and the time periods of morning and evening. According to Chinese philosophy, the communication of eastern and western energy is the pattern of the harmonious state of *Yin* and *Yang*, the way of creation. Thus in Chinese, *Dongxi* 東西 stands for things. *Dongxi* holds the dynamic meaning of a thing established already—because the energy of the East and the energy of the West have worked together to make something, to establish something. *Dongxi* does not mean direction.

I think that starting with the knowledge of *Dongxi* is a good way to share my story because I came to the West (America) from the East (China). Let us enjoy this last cup of tea. Please drink it slowly, if you like. I need to take time to tell you my story.

3.1 *Ming* 命 (Destiny) —My Life

In Chinese, *Ming* 命 means life, destiny, nominate, existence, or command. Now I can talk about some of the details of my story, especially the information related with my *Ming* 命 —destiny or karmic life—my path in this lifetime.

3.1.1 *Xun* 巽 —A Trigram

My hometown in southeast China is right near the Eastern Ocean (which is part of the Pacific Ocean). This is the place where dawn first reaches China. In fact, my hometown is famous for this. This place belongs to the trigram *Xun* 巽, according to the *Yijing* (Book of Changes). *Xun* means wind, wood, or breath and *Ming* 命 means destiny. I want to give some information on *Xun* because everyone's life is related to *Xun* and I have strong *Xun Qi* 气 (energy) in my body, according to my Chinese astrological chart.

In *Yijing* science, *Xun* is the symbol for wind. Wind belongs to the Wood element. The attribute of Wind is the ability to proceed and to propagate gently. It manifests *Qi*, breath, romantic love, news, order, or discipline. Wood, also linked to the East, is a symbol for vitality and life energy, and it has strong momentum. Chapter 76 of the Yellow Emperor's Classic of Medicine states that Wind is produced in the East. In the realm of Heaven, the presence of spirit expresses and manifests itself in the form of Wind. In the Earth, spirit expresses itself in the lushness and aliveness of Wood (plants). The quality of Wood is warm, vibrant, and expansive. The virtues of Wood are peace and harmony. The eminent *Tang* 唐 Dynasty (617–907 CE) physician-scholar *Wang Bing* 王冰 noted that the virtue of Wood is to gently push and advance the expansion of harmonious *Qi*. As Wood emerges, Fire gets stronger and Water, which is symbolic of *Jing* 精 (essence), transforms into *Qi*.[14] This is a pattern of *Qigong* processing. In *Qigong* practice, we will apply *Xun* 巽—Wind—the breathing techniques, to strengthen Fire, our life energy, and change our karmic lives into a better state.

As a child, I was frail and began practicing *Qigong* and *Taiji* at a young age. Inspired by the immediate strengthening effects of this practice, I understood that we can be in command of our destiny rather than succumbing to fate. This is an important Daoist concept: "*Wo Ming Zai Wo Bu Zai Tian* 我命在我不在天" —My life is not controlled by fate alone. My life is in my own hands rather than in the hands of destiny. Believe you have a karmic life and you will find a way to shift your life to a *Xu* state of peace and harmony. I hope my story can inspire you to find your karmic life and start your own spiritual journey.

3.1.2 *Dong* 東 (East) — My Hometown

I was born in the East and grew up there, but over time my practice and my life have been shifting to the West. My elementary school was in my hometown, which was an old lifestyle town—no electricity, no running water, no buses, no cars. My hometown is a fishing village called *Ruoshan* 箬山. When I was growing up there, men went out to fish and women stayed home and took care of the children and family. *Yang* (man) was in charge of the outside (work) and *Yin* (woman) was in charge of the inside (home). This is the natural functioning of *Yin* and *Yang*.[15] The women planted vegetables for self-sufficiency. Water was carried directly from the well because there was no running water. Each of the surrounding villages had its own temple. There were both Buddhist and Taoist temples and the two religions were mixed together. There was also an ancient nature religion. Because the villagers' income came solely from fishing, there were temples to the Ocean Goddess, too. There was also a dragon temple and the *Great Yu* 禹 (the first emperor of the *Xia* 夏 Dynasty) temple (See Part I, 3.2.1 *Ding* 鼎 (Cauldron) — A Symbol for Establish). People believed in nature gods or goddesses and incorporated them into daily life. There were also shamans who helped people, cured sickness, and performed special rituals to ask for a peaceful life.

I grew up in that ancient cultural environment, in the eastern place, and it was there I started my initial practice of cultivation which included chanting, meditation, martial arts, *Qigong*, mystical experiences, and explorations of nature. Then I grew up and started moving west.

3.1.3 *Xi* 西 (West) — My Path

The first western place far away from my hometown was *Xian* 西安. When I was 18 years old, I went away to college in *Xian*, one of the oldest cities in China. Have you heard of the ancient Terracotta Army? Yes, this same city is famous for it. Coming to *Xian* was not my choice. It was more like the universal arrangement.

When I graduated from high school, I had to pass the national exam like everyone else in order to get into college. In China, there were three levels of college. Usually, students were placed into college according to their scores on the national exam. Students with the high scores had the chance to attend one of the best colleges. If they passed the exam with a low score, then they had the chance to go to one of the lowest level colleges. If they didn't pass the exam, then they were not eligible to attend any college at all. This is still the way it is in China. Passing the college exam meant that life would be stable—a free education, a job after graduation, and life-long employment in that job. (This system started changing to a more western style around 10 years ago. Students have to pay tuition now, and it is possible to buy the required score to enter a university.)

At the time I was applying for college, we had to fill out some paperwork and indicate the college we wanted to go to before taking the national exam. My English and my political science were not very good at that time, but my mathematics and other subjects were better. I filled out the papers to choose a college, and as a joke I picked a college in the Northwest, thinking I didn't really have a chance of getting in.

After taking the test, I was surprised to find out I had gotten a very high score and had passed the requirement for getting into one of the best colleges. This meant I had to go to *Xian* in northwest China. (Actually it's in the center of China but is considered northwest from my hometown.) This was around 1,500 miles from my home.

I spent four years in college studying Information Technology Engineering. College life was not difficult for me. In fact, I had more chances to travel and visit my masters to expand my spiritual cultivation. I started teaching my *Qigong* classes in 1988.

I graduated from college in 1989 and expected to have to return to my home-town since that was the government policy then. After the *Tiananmen* Square events on June 4th, the government instituted a law requiring all college students to return to their hometowns after graduating unless they were offered a job elsewhere. The government would find jobs for all the college graduates, and students had a limited choice about where they could go. This was the most important time because we had to find a good place to go. We could request a particular place or region and maybe we could go, but once we were there, we had to stay in that place for our whole lives. There was almost no chance of changing the job or the place. Sometimes a husband lived in one city and his wife in another, and they could get together maybe once a year for a month. (Since then, the government policy has changed to a more western style, and now people have more freedom.)

The province I was from didn't have many companies and I knew if I went back there, I would go to a small town and have a small political position in a job not related to my major—as had happened to some of my friends. I went back to my hometown before I made a decision that winter. I went to the local temple to ask the *Yijing* what to do and the answer I received was that I shouldn't worry about my job, that I would get a good job at the last minute. And by coincidence, I found my job in the aerospace industry in *Xian* at the last minute. That's the strong feeling I had. I knew it was not that I had no choice, but that the universe would make the choice for me.

For twelve years, I worked as an engineer in an aerospace institute in *Xian*. I had a good income and a good environment to support my *Qigong* and spiritual cultivation. I was able to continue my cultivation, envision my future, continue my travels around China, visit hermits, and publish my *Qigong* and martial arts books. Sometimes I did workshops for people, traveling to different provinces and cities and giving lectures during my holidays and vacations. Also, I opened *Qigong* classes for local people in the *Xian* area. Sometimes, I taught courses for international groups that came to China to study with me. In 1993, I started my *Qigong* school and ran it for almost three years while I continued to work as an engineer. My students met with me for teachings and then practiced by themselves at home. I met with them once or twice a year. (I continue this traditional teaching style here in the U.S.) Then in 2001, I came further west to America, moving again from East to West.

3.2 *Yin* 因 (Reason) — Why I am Here

In Chinese, *Yin* 因 means reason, cause. My story is about a journey from the East to the West, and I will tell you why I am here. However, let's first take one more look at the Chinese character *Ding* 鼎. It may help us better understand the reason I am here.

3.2.1 *Ding* 鼎 (Cauldron) — A Symbol for Establish

The Chinese character *Ding* 鼎 means cauldron. Precious bronze cauldrons or alchemical vessels—*Ding*— from over 3,500 years ago can be seen in the collections of many museums. *Ding* is a vessel with three legs and two "ears" (handles). The *Ding* was used, according to the second-century dictionary *Shuowen Jiezi* 說文解字, to "harmonize the five flavors," metaphorically referring to the process of cooking.

The *Ding* is a symbol for ancient China. It is said that over 4,000 years ago, the founder of the *Xia* 夏 Dynasty, Emperor *Dayu* 大禹 (Great Yu), saved China from a great flood by digging an elaborate system of waterways. He separated China into nine states and then cast nine cauldrons—*Ding*—to represent each state. Since those mythical times, every emperor of China has cast a new *Ding* at the beginning of his dynasty as a way to mark and symbolize the new era. Thus the word *Ding* also came to signify power and establishment.[16]

The physical structure of the *Ding*, with its legs, body, and ears, mirrors the human body. The three legs that are characteristic of a *Ding* represent stability or creation. The number three itself has many important connotations. From a Daoist perspective, three is the number of creation and accomplishment. (See Part II, 5.4 *Sancai* 三才 /3— Three Sources.)

A bronze cauldron from the *Shang* Dynasty.

As discussed earlier, the pattern of the universe is made up of three layers: Heaven, Earth, and the Human Being. The Human Being living in this world is connected with these three types of energy. When we want to do something, in order to be successful, three right conditions must be present to help us achieve the goal. The Chinese talk about this situation with a proverb: "*San Zu Ding Li* 三足鼎立"—With three legs, a *Ding* (cauldron) can be set up. These conditions are: *Tianshi* 天時 (right timing), *Dili* 地利 (right place), and *Renhe* 人和 (right companions):

(1) ***Tianshi*** —In Chinese, *Tian* means Heaven and *Shi* means time. *Tianshi* means Heavenly timing or the right timing. We have the ability to do the things we want, but we won't be able to accomplish them if the timing is wrong. The timing is important—and it is called Heavenly timing.

(2) ***Dili***—*Di* means Earth and *Li* means benefit. *Dili* means the benefit from the Earth. In other words, we have the right environment and the right place, and because of this we can accomplish our goals. If the timing is right but we are not in the right place, we won't be able to accomplish our goals.

(3) ***Renhe***—*Ren* means human being and *He* means harmony. *Renhe* means we have a good group of people who can support each other and help us complete our missions. If we don't have this third right condition, we won't be able to do it.

3.2.2 Lucky Element and Three Conditions

Now, let's continue my story. In my Chinese astrology chart, West or Metal is my lucky element according to the Five Elements principle (see Part II 5.6 *Wuxing* 五行 /5 — Five Elements) and it is my place of accomplishment. This element can help me be more balanced and can bring my potential energy out to accomplish my goals. I came here because it is the right time for me to be here. It is the right place for me to be. I can achieve what I want to achieve.

I am writing my first *Qigong* book in English. Let us use it as an example to learn why I am here. As we just discussed, to be successful a person needs three right conditions. Are these three conditions present for my book?

First, let's consider *Tianshi*, right timing. Last year (2004) was the right timing for me to start this book. It was the Year of the Monkey, but there is more to it than that. In Chinese cosmology, space and time are related. Different times are related to different directions and are also related to different elements. Monkey is related to the west direction and belongs to the Metal element. Monkey stands for autumn and the time period 3:00-5:00 pm. Actually, the time I came to America was the right timing as well. The year was 2001, a *Yin* Metal year. My departure time from China was 3:00 p.m. and my arrival time in Portland was 4:00 p.m. Both of these times belong to the Metal element.

There would have been no way to write and publish this book if I had not come here at that time. In 2000 when I was writing my last *Qigong* book in Chinese, the publishing house was given the policy by the government that it was not allowed to use the word "*Qigong*" anywhere in the books it published. Although my book was nearly done, I had to go through all the pages and change all appearances of "*Qigong*" to "Nourishing Life." It was lucky that the book was published at all.

A few months after my book was published, I was told that books of this type could no longer be published, even if the word *Qigong* were changed to something else. Also at that time, the Chinese government stopped all public *Qigong* classes, group *Qigong* practice, activities of *Qigong* organizations, and publications of *Qigong* magazines and journals. (I was happy to learn that the Chinese government started to allow people to learn medical *Qigong* in 2004.) Of course, I wanted to continue my *Qigong* teaching and writing, and in the meantime, I was offered a great opportunity to come to the U.S. to continue my dream.

Second, let's look at *Dili*, right place. Now I am located in the West (specifically, the Pacific Northwest in the United States). I am receiving the Earthly benefits of living here. I do not think I could do my writing in the East (China) where I came from even though now is the right timing. If I had stayed in China, I would not have been able to do any spiritual teaching or help people through *Qigong*. One reason for this is that China is developing its economy and

and most people there are more focused on the material world than on spiritual cultivation. Also, the government has made a strong policy to limit people in their *Qigong* practice and spiritual cultivation.

Third, let's think about *Renhe*, right companions. Most of my students here are Westerners (Metal element). I support them and have gotten much support from them. I am glad that I made a right decision in coming here. In the West, people have more freedom to practice spiritual cultivation. I can share the Chinese wisdom traditions with people here. I have several dedicated groups from all over the world who study with me every year. I am surrounded by many good people who help me harmonize my teaching and my writing (see Acknowledgements). I also have a good publisher to help me bring my book out into the world.

As you can see, the three conditions are present—the right timing, the right place, and the right companions—the best conditions for me to write my book.

3.3 *Guo* 果 (Fruit) — A Drop of Water

In Chinese, *Guo* 果 literally means fruit, and it stands for result. The result of my path so far has been to move me from the East to the West so I would have the chance to teach my *Qigong* and to publish my articles and books. The reason I chose writing and teaching as the goals of my life is that from my personal experience in working with patients, I've found that their physical problems are related to their mental and spiritual bodies. Through my teaching and writing, I am trying to convey this important connection. I want to help people understand that various diseases are related not just to the physical body but are also related to the spiritual heart. To recover from disease or imbalances, the majority of patients need to do spiritual cultivation in addition to physical treatment.

Perhaps this book can inspire more people to follow the wisdom of classical spiritual cultivation. My hope is that my book will be like a small drop of water falling into the ocean, making ripples that resonate with people's hearts. I hope this drop of water will facilitate the awakening of consciousness for many people. I humbly pray that more true masters drop their "jade" (wisdom) into the *Qi* Ocean to make huge ripples that will guide you on your spiritual journey.

PART II

Han San He Yi

含三合一

Holding Three in One

The Fundamentals of
Chinese Shamanic *Qigong*

Three Gives Birth to the Ten Thousand Things[1]

三生萬物

San Sheng Wan Wu

The ancient *Wu* (shamans) understood that three is the universal number of creation. Trinity, a group of three in one, is one of the most important concepts in the Chinese shamanic spiritual traditions. The *Yijing* (*I Ching* or Book of Changes) contains three secret and sacred layers of wisdom: *Xiang* 象 (symbolism), *Shu* 數 (numerology), and *Li* 理 (theory). Since the *Yijing* is considered to be the root of classical Chinese science and civilization, it can also be used to gain deeper insights into the foundation of *Qigong* theory[2]. Therefore, in Part II, we will discuss how *Xiang, Shu*, and *Li* inform the basic *Qigong* principles.

象 *Xiang*

Symbolism

In Chinese, the original meaning of *Xiang* 象 was elephant. The elephant is the largest beast in the world and can be easily recognized by its physical features. Elephants were numerous in the central area of ancient China; in fact, the oldest Chinese character for elephant looks like a picture of an elephant. A natural phenomenon is as easy to recognize as the shape of an elephant; thus, *Xiang* also means phenomenon or symbol. Ancient Chinese shamans used symbols as vehicles to access different universal energies. In Chinese shamanic *Qigong* practice, we still use these techniques for self-cultivation and for healing others. In this section, we will learn about some aspects of *Xiang* culture, including totemism, myth, and the symbolic meaning of the tiger. This may inspire us to begin our inner cultivation.

Yellow River ancient elephant fossil; discovered in *Gansu* Province 甘肃省 in 1973. This ancient elephant lived about 25,000,000 years ago.

4.1 *Tuteng* 圖騰 (Totemism) — Between Heaven and Earth

4.1.1 The Nature of *Tuteng*

Actually, the Chinese character *Xiang* 象 is similar in meaning to totem. In the 1920's, some Chinese scholars started applying Western research tools to investigate ancient Chinese culture. The Native American term "totem" was first introduced into Chinese at that time. It was translated into phonetic Chinese as *Tuteng* 圖騰. Before I discovered this, I thought that *Tuteng* was an original Chinese term used in the study of the wisdom traditions of ancient Chinese tribes and shamanism. I made this mistake because the two Chinese characters 圖騰 carry a meaning similar to totem. Let us take a few minutes to learn some of the meanings of these two characters.

Tu 圖 means picture, chart, drawing, or map. Its original meanings were intention, attempt, plan, design, or territory. This character is an image of a person facing, and giving careful consideration to, an important issue: the delineation of personal space or territory. In totemism, territory is a vital concept. As totems, animals and planets always hold their space. For instance, after the rain, the first thing the African lion does is to rebuild its territory by marking the boundaries with its own bodily waste (urine and feces). In our spiritual cultivation, one important technique is to hold our space.

The character *Teng* 騰 is an image of a horse galloping. This image carries the idea of clearing out, jumping, rising, soaring, fast speed, override, or transfer. In shamanic tradition, the horse is a symbol for Heaven and Spirit. One of the inner cultivation processes is to lift and elevate your spirit. I think the Chinese scholars picked the perfect words to translate totem.

4.1.2 Chinese Totemism

There were many tribes in ancient China and most of them had their own languages and totems. There are still more than fifty tribes in modern China.

Modern archeology tells us that the flower was one of the ancient matriarchal tribe totems in central China near Flower Mountain (*Huashan* 華山). Scholars believe that the ancient flower totem is the source of the original name for China, *Zhonghua* 中華, which literally means central flower. The Chinese totem pole is named *Huabiao* 華表 – literally meaning flower tablet. It is the symbol for the Chinese nation. In traditional

Flower pattern on pottery; from about 5,600 years ago.

Chinese spiritual cultivation, the flower is the symbol for the transcendent essential energies of the body.

The bird was one of the earliest totems in ancient China. Archeologists discovered this totem in different areas of China and discovered that the matriarchal bird tribe used to be the leader of all the tribes in ancient times. In the Chinese shamanic tradition, the bird is the symbol for the spirit of the body.

The Chinese totem pole is named Huabiao–literally meaning flower tablet.

Bronze totem with a human face and bird body from one of the ancient Chinese Shamanic Kingdoms in *Sichuan* 四川 Province; from about 4,000 years ago.

Gold carving of four birds encircling the sun; from about 3,500 years ago.

Of course, the dragon and the tiger were also common totems in ancient China. The dragon tribe was located in Eastern China and the tiger tribe was located in Western China. Approximately 5,000—6,000 years ago, these two tribes took over the leadership of all the tribes. It was said that 5,000 years ago *Huangdi* 黃帝 (Yellow Emperor) led his dragon tribe in war against the *Yandi* 炎帝 (Fire Emperor) tiger tribe in Central China. After a big battle, the two tribes united. Later, *Huangdi* continued to unite more tribes. (The Chinese regard these two emperors as their ancestors). In Chinese shamanic tradition, the dragon represents East, Liver, and rising *Yang* energy while the tiger represents West, Lung, and descending *Yin* energy. The union of *Yin* and *Yang* energies is called "the union of the tiger and the dragon."

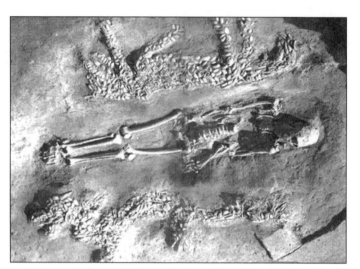

Sculptures of a dragon and a tiger made of seashells and placed on either side of a shaman's skeleton; from 6,400 years ago in *Henan* 河南 Province.

There were many more totems in ancient China such as the fish, bear, deer, frog, boar/pig, and tree, although we will not discuss them here. We will learn more details about the tiger totem in Part II, 4.3 *Laohu* 老虎 (Tiger) - Vital Breath since this book is about Shamanic Tiger *Qigong*.

4.2 *Shenhua* 神話 (Myth) – The Union of Humans and Spirits

In Chinese, *Shen* 神 means spirit, infinite, magic, marvelous, deity, or divine. *Hua* 話 means speak, talk, tell, speech, or story. Literally, *Shenhua* 神話 means a story about spirits or gods, and it also means Chinese myths or mythology. There were many ancient *Shenhua* (myths) in Chinese shamanism. Actually, *Shenhua* is a doorway to the divine, and the deities in a myth are embodiments of different levels of consciousness or spirits. Studying mythology is a way to awaken our consciousness and inner spirits. I will share three myths with you.

4.2.1 *Xiwangmu* 西王母 — Queen Mother of the West

Xiwangmu 西王母, the Queen Mother of the West, was first seen in *Shanhaijing* 山海經 (The Canon of Mountains and Seas). This book contains three descriptions of *Xiwangmu*.

First, the Western Great Remote (*Dahuangxijing* 大荒西經) section of The Canon of Mountains and Seas tells us:

Stone carving of the Queen Mother of the West; from an early *Han* Dynasty tomb.

In the south of the West Sea, on the bank of the Sandy River, in back of the Red Water and in front of the Black Water, there is a great mountain named *Kunlun*. On this mountain, there is a deity with a human face and a tiger body, and the body has white stripes and a tail. This deity wears a *Xing* 勝 (jade flower) and has tiger teeth and a leopard tail. She dwells in a cave and her name is *Xiwangmu* 西王母. Everything is in this mountain.[3]

Second, the West Mountain (*Xishanjing* 西山經) section of the same book tells us:

Yushan 玉山 (Jade Mountain) is the dwelling place of the *Xiwangmu* 西王母. Her shape is human-like with a leopard tail and tiger teeth. She is adept at whistling. She wears a *Xing* 勝 (jade flower) in her loosened hair. She holds the universal power of punishment over everything.[4]

Third, the North of the Inner Sea (*Haineibeijing* 海内北經) section of the book tells us:

On Snake Shaman Mountain, there is someone who holds a peach-wood scepter and faces the eastern direction, although some say she lives on Tortoise Mountain. She is *Xiwangmu* 西王母 (the Queen Mother of the West). She stands on the terrace holding a staff of power and wearing a *Xing* 勝 (jade flower). To her south are three green birds that gather food for her. This is to the north of *Kunlunxu* 崐崘虛 (Void or Cave).[5]

The Queen Mother of the West is a condensation of the Subtlest Vital Breath of the Western Essence from the Vital Breath of the Dao of the Primordial Chaos (Cosmos). This deity, surnamed *Hou* 侯, is allocated the western direction. Figures of a human body with tiger teeth, a white tiger body, and a leopard tail were considered envoys of the Queen Mother of the West and the White Tiger spirit of the West. This image was more a symbol of her shamanic power than simply a representation of the Queen Mother of the West herself. The peach-wood staff mentioned here is not a walking stick but a decorative ornament used to connect with the universe. According to shamanic tradition, a staff has the power to drive off demons.

Tales have portrayed the Queen Mother of the West as both majestic and unreasonable. In ancient books, however, she is described as an intriguing beauty who remains forever in the first flush of youth due to her discovery of the elixir of immortality. Historical annals from the *Han* 漢 Dynasty, *Shiji* 史記, record that the Queen Mother of the West appeared as a virtuous, compassionate, ageless beauty during the reigns of *Huangdi* 黃帝 (Yellow Emperor), King *Mu* 穆 of the *Zhou* 周 Dynasty, and Emperor *Wu* 武 of the *Han* 漢 Dynasty.

In the perspective of the Daoist religion, the Queen Mother of the West rules over the Western Paradise and is the head of a pantheon of goddesses and female immortals. The Queen Mother of the West lives in the *Kunlun* 崐崘 Mountains in a city that spans one thousand miles and has twelve jade mansions with halls of green light, nine-story primordial chambers, and purple and green elixir chambers. To the left is the Jade Lake and to the right are the Green Mountains. In her garden, she grows the peaches of immortality. According to the *Bowuzhi* 博物志 (*Natural Science and Miscellaneous Stories*), the peach trees by the Jade Lake "bear fruit once every 3,000 years."

The different images of the Queen Mother of the West symbolize an infinite feminine universal force as well as immortality. In shamanic tradition, she represents the prenatal consciousness of the body which originated in the Dao.

4.2.2 *Pangu* 盘古 — the Giant

In China, we have a creation story:[6]

In the beginning, Heaven and Earth were still one and all was chaos. The universe was like a big egg. The giant *Pangu* slept inside this egg. All was dark. After 18,000 years, he awoke, became anxious, and flailed his limbs until the egg broke. Suddenly, light streamed in. The clear part of this light floated up and formed Heaven. The cold, turbid matter stayed below to form Earth.

Stone carving of *Pangu*, from a *Han* Dynasty tomb.

Pangu stood up and stretched. His hands held up Heaven and his feet stood on Earth. Heaven and Earth began to grow and *Pangu* grew along with them to support the two. After another 18,000 years, the sky was higher, the Earth thicker, and *Pangu* stood between them like a huge pillar so that they would never be joined again.

When *Pangu* died, his breath became the wind and clouds and his voice became the rolling thunder. His left eye became the sun while his right eye became the moon. His body and limbs turned into the five sacred mountains and his blood formed the rivers and oceans. His muscles transformed into the soil. The innumerable stars in the sky came from his hair, and grass and trees grew from his skin and the fine hairs on his body. His bone marrow turned into jade and pearls.

The egg is analogous to the Dao—the Oneness. The prenatal self simply exists inside the *Qi*—like *Pangu* resting inside the egg. The postnatal body represents a breaking through and a separation; however, we can still be connected to Heaven and Earth through the *Qi*. Heavenly and Earthly phenomena all come from the *Qi*. Likewise, our bodies—eyes, bones, and blood—come from the *Qi*. In Chinese shamanic tradition, *Pangu* symbolizes the rooted ancestral spirit of the body. This spiritual energy enables a human being to stand up with confidence and strength and to never give up in the face of possible failure.

4.2.3 *Hundun* 渾沌 – The Chaos

Hundun means chaos, one mass, or non-separation. In Chinese cosmology and mythology, *Hundun* normally means the Primordial Cosmos. The famous Daoist master *Zhuangzi* 莊子 (approximately 369—295 BCE) had a story about *Hundun*:

> The emperor of South Sea was *Shu* 儵 (Go Fast), the emperor of North Sea was *Hu* 忽 (Come Swiftly), and the Central emperor was *Hundun* 渾沌 (Primordial Cosmos). Customarily, *Shu* and *Hu* got together in *Hundun's* territory and *Hundun* always treated them as his most hon-ored guests. One day, *Shu* and *Hu* planned what they thought was the best way to repay *Hundun* for his kindness: "All of us have seven ori-fices through which we can see, hear, eat, and breathe. Only *Hundun* has none of these orifices. Let us make them for him." Then *Shu* and *Hu* started to chisel orifices on *Hundun*. Each day they made one orifice on *Hundun*. On the seventh day, *Hundun* died.

Here, *Shu* represents the postnatal *Shen* 神 (spirit/mind) of the Heart and *Hu* stands for the postnatal *Jing* 精 (essence) of the Kidney. *Hundun* symbolizes the primordial *Shen* 神 (spirit/consciousness) of the body. The orifices are the ener-getic windows of our desires. Seeing, hearing, eating, and breathing create our desires and these activities make our energy leak through our orifices, which are the pathways to death. It is very important to shut off these spiritual win-dows to move back to the *Hundun* state in our spiritual cultivation.

4.3. *Laohuo* 老虎 (Tiger) — Vital Breath

4.3.1 The Power of the Tiger

The tiger is a very powerful animal, protected by the strength of its skin, its weapons of "iron teeth and metal claws,"[7] its thunderous growl, and its ferocity. The tiger has the power to drive out *Yin* (demons and diseases). In Chinese shamanic tradition, the striped pattern of the tiger skin represents the Dao. The tiger is the king of the beasts and has a pattern on his forehead that looks like

Stone tiger with cinnabar in its mouth, eyes, and ears; from about 4,000 years ago. In Chinese shamanic tradition, the function of cinnabar is to release evil energy.

the Chinese character *Wang* 王, which means king. In ancient Chinese tradition, kings, generals, and judges were often depicted as officiating from chairs that were ceremoniously draped with a tiger skin. Chinese shamans often donned tiger skins and tiger masks for exorcism rituals. Warriors regularly used tiger skins on their shields, armor, and helmets to intimidate the enemy. Chinese living rooms often feature tiger images to drive out evil influences. "The tiger devours demons and evil spirits. Therefore, when people meet with bad fortune, they incinerate a tiger skin and drink the ashes or they touch a tiger claw, which can also drive out evil influences."[8]

When you read Part III *Laohu Gong* 老虎功 – Chinese Shamanic Tiger *Qigong* Form, you may find you can really feel the martial power of the tiger. Through this martial power, you can learn how to respond to your "enemy." This is also

Jade tiger; from 4,000 years ago.

true for *Qigong* in its medical function. It is a way to learn how to work with disease by using your inner power.

4.3.2 The Symbolic Tiger

As a totem that corresponds to the great Dao, the tiger holds numerous symbolic meanings. I will list only those that are related to Part III: Lung, breath, *Qi* 气, respiration system, change, control, circulation, rule, rhythm, West, Metal, Venus, transparency, upright, justice, autumn, wind, the Queen Mother of the West, and the seven Chinese lunar mansions in the Western sky.

Generally, in Chinese shamanic tradition, the tiger is addressed as *Baihu* 白虎—White Tiger. In Chinese culture, white does not merely mean the color white; rather, it is the symbol for transparency, clarity, purification, justice, or punishment, and is also symbolic of the activities of killing and destruction. The symbol for white is equal to the spiritual quality of the tiger totem. In nature, we can learn about the spiritual White Tiger through the "killing" atmosphere of the fall season. This killing is the process that generates new life in the spring season and is the natural way to clear out old energy and weakness and to maintain stronger life energy.

As we observe in nature, when autumn comes, strong wind not only sweeps down the leaves from the trees but also breaks down the weak and sick branches of the trees. When the next spring comes, these trees grow into a better shape. We can discover this natural-spiritual tiger "killing" function of the fall season in the body by learning the function of the Lung. Regular Lung function breaks down old energy (including dead cells), clears up stagnation, kills invading evil (virus), and maintains *Qi* circulation. We would get sick easily without this "killing" function of the Lung.

We can learn much more about the symbolic meanings of the tiger by practicing the Chinese Shamanic Tiger *Qigong* in *Laohu Gong* 老虎功 – Chinese Shamanic Tiger *Qigong* Form.

数 *Shu*

Numerology

5.1 *Wuji* 无极 /0⁹ — The Dao

When I was in middle school, I had a great interest in mathematics. After more than twenty years, I still remember how amazed I was by the magical number zero. It is neither a positive number nor a negative number; it is just itself. Yet, we cannot classify a number as positive or negative without it. In a reference chart, zero is the center or point of origin. From this center point and going in opposite directions, a number will be infinite, large, or small. This function of zero in math is similar to its numerological meaning in *Yijing* science.

In Chinese, zero is *Ling* 零, meaning emptiness. The Chinese character for zero is made with the radical *Yu* 雨 (rain) on top and the radical *Ling* 令 (order) at the bottom. This signifies order or the way of nature. Nature will be filled with abundance and life energy if the rain is in order. Too much rain or not enough rain will cause problems.

We usually use a circle (O) to represent zero. As we discussed in Part I, 2.3 *Kong* 空 (Emptiness) — The Universal Web, emptiness is not equal to nothingness. It is the body of the Dao itself. The original purpose of *Qigong* was to help the practitioner move back into this state of emptiness. This numerological meaning of *Ling*, zero, corresponds to the concept of emptiness, or "*Wuji* 无極 " (no polarity) in classical Chinese philosophy.

Wu means no, nothing, or emptiness. *Ji* means end, limitation, polar, or polarity. Thus, *Wuji* means perfect circulation, without beginning or end. This is the original state of everything. In Chinese, we call it "*Yi Qi Huandun* 一气混沌—one mass of chaotic *Qi* (vital energy). *Laozi* explains that a chaotic *Qi* state is the origin of the universe:

有物混成	*There was something from chaos.*
先天地生	*Before Heaven and Earth, it existed:*
寂兮寥兮	*Silent, isolated,*
獨立而不改	*Standing alone, changing not,*
周行而不殆	*Eternally revolving without fail,*
可以為天下母	*Worthy to be the Mother of All Things.*
吾不知其名	*I do not know its name*
字之曰道	*And address it as Dao.*
強為名之曰大	*If forced to give it a name, I shall call it Great.*[10]

This state before Heaven and Earth is the *Wuji*, or the Dao itself. It is the number *Ling*, zero. From the primordial cosmos until now, it has never changed its way. In general, we may not notice the significance of zero. The Dao is the same as zero. We might not be able to understand what it is until we become enlightened. The great Dao is very close to us, yet we look far away.

The numerological meaning of *Ling* (zero) represents the *Wuji*, or the Dao. The Dao never belongs to anything, but it carries everything. Therefore, the number zero does not belong to any of the elements in the Five Elements principle.

In *Qigong* practice, zero stands for emptiness. We need to purify our physical and spiritual bodies through our *Qigong* practice. It is the same as when we drink tea. We should first empty the cup before pouring in fresh tea and tasting it.

5.2 *Taiji* 太極 /1 — The Universal Life Force

The unity of everything follows the energetic state of *Wuji*, the primordial cosmic *Qi*. *Wuji* generated an inner momentum creating two opposing movements. This is the dynamic *Qi* state of *Taiji*. The literal meaning of *Taiji* is extreme ends or going to the limit. For example, a circle (O) stretched horizontally to the end of its limit will eventually become a straight line (—). In fact, in *Yijing* science, the number one represents *Taiji*.

In Chinese, the number one is written as a horizontal line (—). It has two ends representing the combination of *Yin* and *Yang*. If we cut the

Bronze spiral discovered in *Sichuan* Province; from about 4,000 years ago. The spiral pattern is regarded as an old *Taiji* pattern and was a common totem in ancient China.

line in half, there will be two lines with four ends (— —), but each line still has two ends. In Chinese numerology, the number one, *Yi* (—), is a symbol for unity. It represents stability and harmony.

Just as in human cell division, this process is a symbol of the divisive union in nature. The opposing movement within an individual component is *Taiji*, the oneness of the universe. *Laozi* indicated, *"Fan Zhe Dao Zhi Dong* 反者道之動"
—The opposite way is the motivation of the Dao. The number one is a symbol of the universal life force. It is *Taiji*, the inner force of the existence of the universe.

In the *Yijing*, the numerological meaning of the number one is the water element. Water is the Kidney official of the body. One is the first number of the Five Element numbers. In ancient Chinese cosmology, water was the first element created by the universe. In the *Bamboo Book*, a recording of this idea states, "The Great One gave birth to Water."[11] The Great One refers to the universe.

Both the body (microcosm) and the Earth (macrocosm) contain 70% water. The main technique of *Qigong* is to refine the body's water (*Lianye* 煉液). One of the purposes of *Qigong* practice is to maintain the *Jing* 精 (essence or body fluids) and to move into the state of oneness, uniting oneself with nature. Accordingly, another name for *Qigong* in Chinese is *Shouyi* 守一— holding oneness.

5.3 *Liangyi* 兩儀 /2 — *Yin Yang*

In Classical Chinese, the number two, *Er* 二, is written with two horizontal lines to represent Heaven and Earth. According to ancient Chinese cosmology, the momentum of *Taiji*, the chaotic primordial *Qi*, gave birth to two types of *Qi*: heavy *Qi* and light *Qi*. These two types moved in opposite directions. The heavy *Qi* descended to form the Earth while the light *Qi* rose to form Heaven. *Er* is also pronounced *Liang* and is written as 兩 .

In the *Yijing*, the number two stands for *Yin* and *Yang*, or *Liangyi* 兩 . These terms, *Yin* and *Yang* or *Liangyi*, allow people to understand an object through the expression of opposites. *Bagua* 八卦, the Eight Trigrams, is the foundational knowledge in *Yijing* science. The four pairs of universal *Liangyi* in the *Bagua* are: *Qian* 乾 (Heaven) and *Kun* 坤 (Earth); *Zhen* 震 (Thunder) and *Xun* 巽 (Wind); *Gen* 艮 (Mountain) and *Dui* 兌 (Lake); and lastly, *Kan* 坎 (Water) and *Li* 離 (Fire). Chapter Two of *Laozi's Daodejing* describes this Universal Way as:

有無相生	*Being and non-being create each other.*
難易相成	*Difficult and easy inter-depend in completion.*
長短相形	*Long and short determine one another.*
高下相傾	*High and low distinguish each other.*
音聲相和	*Voice and resonant sound give harmony to one another.*
前後相隨	*Before and after follow each other.*

In *Yijing* numerology, the number two stands for Fire. Fire is represented in our bodies by the Heart. Two is the number for Fire in the Five Element number system, and the number two belongs to the south direction.

In *Qigong* practice, we learn movements, which are *Yang*, and stillness postures, which are *Yin*. We can understand the Dao through understanding *Yin* and *Yang*. Confucius defined the Dao as "one *Yin* and one *Yang* combining."[12]

5.4 *Sancai* 三才 /3 — Three Sources

In Chinese, the number three is *San*. It is written with three horizontal lines to represent the three layers of the universe. The three layers are known as *Sanyuan* 三元, the three sources, or *Sancai* 三才, the three materials. *Sanyuan* and *Sancai* both mean the key components of the universe, which include everything constructed by the three layers. To understand the number three is another way to understand the Dao. This is no coincidence, and it is why the *Yijing* uses three lines to construct a trigram. Each line represents a layer of the universe.

The number three itself has many important connotations. From a Daoist perspective, three is the number of creation and accomplishment. Chapter 42 of the *Daodejing* states:

道生一	*The Dao gives birth to the One,*
一生二	*The One gives birth to the Two,*
二生三	*The Two gives birth to the Three,*
三生萬物	*And the Three gives birth to the Ten Thousand Things.*

The *Shuowen Jiezi* also explains three as being "the Dao of Heaven, Earth, and Humanity." These three aspects can be further subdivided into threes: Heaven has three lights: the sun, the moon, and the stars. Earth has three sources of energy: water, fire, and wind. Humans have three treasures: *Jing, Qi,* and *Shen*. According to the sages, we can strengthen our own *Jing, Qi,* and *Shen* by communicating with the three Heavenly lights and the three sources of

Earth energy. The Yellow Emperor's Classic of Medicine (*Huangdi Neijing*) states, "If one understands the Dao of Heaven, Earth, and Humanity and follows the Dao, one will live a long life" (Chapter 78).[13]

The number three represents the creation of the universe. In the *Yijing*, three is the Dao (the Way) of Heaven, Earth, and the Human Being. According to ancient Chinese cosmology, after Heaven and Earth were formed from the Primordial *Qi* (*Wuji*), the *Qi* of Heaven and the *Qi* of Earth were attracted to each other because they both came from the same source. Therefore, Heaven's *Qi* descended and Earth's *Qi* rose, meeting each other in the middle, between Heaven and Earth. These movements of Heavenly and Earthly *Qi* gave birth to everything in the universe. The *Yijing* explains this as: "The intercourse of Heaven and Earth gives birth to the Ten Thousand Things." The Human Being is among the most precious of all the Ten Thousand Things. Thus, the Human Being represents everything between Heaven and Earth. This is the pattern of the creation of the universe. The number three, then, refers to the three layers of the universe.

In the Five Element number system, the number three belongs to the Wood element. Three stands for the Liver in the body and belongs to the eastern direction. It represents the universal life force. In *Qigong* practice, we always work with three: posture, breath, and visualization. This is the way to strengthen and harmonize the three treasures of the body: *Jing* (essence), *Qi* (vital energy), and *Shen* (spirit).

5.5 *Sixiang* 四象/4 — Four Universal Spiritual Animals

In Chinese, the number four is *Si* 四. It stands for the four directions of the universe: East, West, South, and North. Similarly, it stands for the concept of space. In *Yijing* science, the number four is equal to four symbols, the *Sixiang* in Chinese. These four symbols are related to the four spiritual animals in the sky: *Qinglong* 青龍 Green Dragon in the East, *Baihu* 白虎 White Tiger in the West, *Zhuque* 朱雀 Red Bird in the South, and *Xuanwu* 玄武 Black Warrior in the North. Four is also symbolic of time and refers to the four seasons of the year.

Wall painting of Green Dragon; from 1,800 years ago.

Wall painting of White Tiger; from 1,800 years ago.

Wall painting of Black Warrior; from 1,800 years ago.

Wall painting of Red Bird; from 1,800 years ago.

In discussing the number two, we defined *Liangyi* as the expression of *Yin* and *Yang*. In the *Yijing*, these *Liangyi* are drawn as one continuous line to represent *Yang* while one divided line represents *Yin*. The relative nature of *Yin* and *Yang* combinations produced the *Sixiang*, or four pictures. The *Sixiang* are produced from combining the maximum number of possible combinations of these lines: *Taiyang* (Great *Yang*), composed of two *Yang* lines; *Shaoyang* (Lesser *Yang*), composed of one *Yin* line on the bottom and one *Yang* line on the top; *Shaoyin* (Lesser *Yin*), composed of one *Yang* line on the bottom and one *Yin* line on the top; and *Taiyin* (Great *Yin*), composed of two broken *Yin* lines. The *Bagua*, or Eight Trigrams, was created in the same fashion of possible combinations from the *Sixiang*. (See Part II, 5.9 *Bagua* 八卦/8 — Trigram)

The shape of the Chinese character *Si* 四 (four) is square. Square is the symbol for Earth. According to ancient Chinese mythology, four pillars on Earth support Heaven.[14] These four pillars are the four limbs of the body. The human being is the microcosm of the macrocosm of the universe. Thus, the physical body is the "Earth" of a person, while the spirit is the "Heaven" of a person. In *Qigong* practice, we use our four pillars, or limbs, to unite our Heaven and Earth, our physical and spiritual bodies.

Other meanings for the number four in Chinese include balance and harmony. Traditional Chinese wedding gifts are related to the number four. Parents and friends give four gifts to the bride and groom as a way to bless their marriage, filling it with peace, love, and stability.

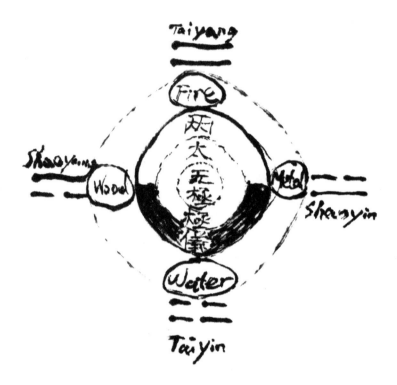

According to the numerology of the *Yijing, Si* (four) is the number for the Metal element. Four belongs to the western direction and correlates with the Lung in our bodies. Just as the four seasons are the rhythm of nature, so the Lung is in charge of the rhythm of our life force.

5.6 *Wuxing* 五行 /5 — Five Elements

In Chinese, five is *Wu* 五. The oracle bone style for five is a symbol to represent the *Yin* and *Yang* energies interacting and dancing between Heaven and Earth. This is the pattern of peace, balance, and health.

In *Yijing* science, the number five stands for *Wuxing*, the Five Elements of the universe. *Wuxing*, the Five Element Theory, is the essence of classical Chinese philosophy. The three layers of the universe are constructed of the Five

Elements: Water, Fire, Wood, Metal, and Earth. The word *Xing* that is translated as "element" here actually means movement, change, or development. Each movement has its *Yin* and *Yang* aspect and each should be in balance. In a balanced environment, we will live peacefully and feel lucky.

Wu

The energies of the Five Elements are also reflected in the Five Planets: Mercury represents Water, Jupiter represents Wood, Mars represents Fire, Saturn represents Earth, and Venus represents Metal.

Since the human being is part of the universe, understanding the Five Element principle is a way to understand our bodies. With this principle, a Chinese medicine doctor may discern what sort of disease a patient may have. Further, the doctor will apply this principle to help the patient find a proper way to avoid disease or recover from an existing disease.

From the Chinese shamanic perspective, the body is an energetic system constructed of five subsystems: Liver, Heart, Spleen, Lung, and Kidney. Each subsystem represents one of the Five Elements and connects with one of the five directions. Please check the Five Elements Chart below for details.

五行 *Five Elements Chart*

5 Elements	Metal	Water	Wood	Fire	Earth
Direction	West	North	East	South	Center
Planet	Venus	Mercury	Jupiter	Mars	Saturn
Organ	Lungs	Kidneys	Liver	Heart	Spleen
Color	White (Golden)	Black	Green	Red	Yellow
Flavor	Spicy	Salty	Sour	Bitter	Sweet
Fruit	Peach	Chestnut	Plum	Apricot	Date
Season	Fall	Winter	Spring	Summer	Four Seasons
System	Respiratory	Excretory	Nervous	Circulatory	Digestive
Body Layer	Skin	Bone	Nerves	Blood	Muscle
Face	Nose	Ears	Eyes	Tongue	Mouth
Emotion	Sad	Fear	Anger	Happy	Worry
Disease	Dry	Cold	Wind	Hot	Wet
Personality	Righteous	Gentle	Compassionate	Polite	Trusting

If one of the subsystems of the body has a problem or an imbalance, it will affect the other subsystems and will cause sickness or weight imbalance. One of the goals of *Qigong* practice is to harmonize the Five Element energies in our bodies. The body will be well maintained if the Five Element energies are in a balanced state.

In the Five Element number system, the number five itself (*Wu*) belongs to the Earth element and is likened to Earth's function "to harmonize." Five is the Spleen in the body. As an Earth number, five is the center of the universe. Without a center, we are unable to determine any of the other directions. Therefore, five means coordinator or to nurture. More meanings of five in Chinese include perfect, union, matchmaker, or balance.

5.7 *Liuhe* 六合 / *Liuxu* 六虛 / 6 — Six Unions / Emptiness

Liu

In Chinese, the number six is *Liu*. In oracle bone writing, *Liu* looks like a house. In fact, it is the house of the universe itself. We call the cosmos *Liuxu*, which means six emptinesses, or *Liuhe*, which means six unions. Observing the universe through the center of the body, we note six directions: front, back, left, right, up, and down. Likewise, a hexagram in the *Yijing* is constructed with six lines and represents the way of the universe.

In *Yijing* science, six is a partner of the number one and is the performing number of water. It is *Yin* water and belongs to the Kidney in the microcosm of the human body. Heavenly water performing on the Earth can be seen in the six petals of the snowflake. Thus, six is the symbol of essential *Yin Qi*.

In *Qigong* practice, one of the important procedures is to check the posture. The posture should reflect *Liuhe* (the six unions). This means that the six parts of the body (hands, feet, elbows, knees, shoulders, and hips) should be united. Correct posture in *Qigong* or in martial arts always requires *Liuhe*. When the six parts of the body are united in *Liuhe*, the *Qi* (vital energy) in our bodies follows the pattern of water. In our practice, the movements and energies should flow like water without blockage.

5.8 *Qixing* 七星 /7 — The Big Dipper

In Chinese, the number seven is *Qi* 七. In oracle bone writing, seven is equivalent to ten. Seven is a *Yang* number, holding *Yin* and *Yang* to represent the Dao. In Chinese, seven is identical in pronunciation to the word for lacquer—*Qi* 漆. Lacquer is a coating that functions to protect an object and it is also a symbol for eternity. Lacquer art in China dates back at least 2,000 years.

Lacquer painting discovered in a *Chu* State tomb; from about 2,243 years ago. The symbol in the center of the painting represents the Big Dipper.

曾侯乙墓出土二十八宿漆箱

Qi 七 stands for the central position in the *Yijing*. Further, the central position stands for contractor. In Chinese, this central position, or contractor, refers to the host or the emperor of a country. Seven is equivalent to *Qixing* 七星, or the seven stars in the Big Dipper. According to *Wu* (Chinese shamanic tradition), the Big Dipper is the Heart of Heaven. The ancient shamans read the beating of this Heart, or observed the movement of the handle of the Big Dipper, to foretell changes in the Universal *Qi*. The Big Dipper is considered to be the chariot of the Heavenly Emperor, and through changes in the handling of this chariot, the Heavenly Emperor controls the changes of the four seasons of the year.

In *Yijing* numerology, the number seven is the pattern of two and the element of Fire. Seven belongs to the Heart in the microcosm of the body while the *Qixing* 七星 (seven stars of the Big Dipper) represent the seven orifices of

Stone carving of the Big Dipper chariot; from early *Han* Dynasty.

the head. The seven orifices consist of two eyes, two ears, two nostrils, and one mouth. In *Qigong* practice, it is important to know how to work with the seven orifices because they are related to the emperor, or Heart, in the body. *Shen* (spirit) resides in the Heart.

In Chinese cosmology, seven represents the infinite space and time of the universe. In the *Yijing*, seven stands for rebirth or re-creation, as the hexagram *Fu* beckons to "...repeat the Way, [*Yang Qi* will] return after seven days."

The story of *Hundun* told by Daoist Master *Zhuangzi* may inspire our spiritual cultivation (see Part II, 4.2.3 *Hundun* 渾沌 – The Chaos).

5.9 *Bagua* 八卦 /8 — Trigram

In Chinese, the number eight is *Ba*. In oracle bone style writing, the number eight is illustrated as a pattern of division. The character *Ba* 八 depicts two lines dividing. In classical Chinese, eight means separation, or to separate. Separation is a way of change, according to *Yijing* philosophy, because hidden within the concept of separation is the meaning of cooperation for the next step of creation. As we discussed with the number three (a number of creation), the trigrams with their three lines representing Heaven, Earth, and the Human Being reflect the universal energy. The number three, as a number of creation, gives birth to the universe. Similarly, the number eight, while holding the meaning of separation, also holds the meaning of cooperation and order, which in turn gives rise to creation. This ordered cooperation is demonstrated by modern science, which has mapped cell division in its progression from one cell to two cells to four cells to eight cells.

One pattern of arrangement forms the *Bagua*: prenatal.

This pattern of separation and change is ordered in a certain way to produce creative energy. This is evident in the creation of the *Bagua* (Eight Trigrams) which forms the basis of *Yijing* science. Recall the symbol of *Taiji*, the great primordial momentum of *Yin* and *Yang* yoked together and intertwined to produce continual movement and represented by the number one. Chinese cosmology tells us that separation occurred when the light *Qi* ascended to form Heaven and the heavy *Qi* descended to form the Earth, thus representing the number two.

One pattern of arrangement forms the *Bagua*: postnatal.

Two patterns of arrangement form the *Bagua*: prenatal and postnatal, or Early Heaven and Later Heaven. Put in general terms, the prenatal or Early Heaven arrangement of the *Bagua* reflects the innate energy necessary for creation by the interaction of polar forces. The postnatal or Later Heaven arrangement of the *Bagua* reflects a self-generating cyclic movement. These positions of the Later Heaven arrangement are fixed to represent the Universal Way and the concepts of space and time.

According to ancient Chinese cosmology, the orbits of the planets are circular at 360 degrees. Dividing the degree of orbit by the number eight produces segments of 45 degrees. Each 45-degree segment represents a section of Universal *Qi*, denoting time and space. The *Bagua* is arranged in 45-degree increments to demonstrate this order. Each trigram is located in the space of the eight directions: North, South, East, West, Northeast, Southeast, Southwest, and Northwest. The *Bagua* also holds the meaning of time in terms of season:

winter, summer, spring, fall, winter solstice, summer solstice, spring equinox, and fall equinox. One year of energy coinciding with the planetary orbit is divided into these eight sections and is named *Bajie* 八節.

Knowing now that eight holds the meaning of separation as well as the hidden meaning of cooperation for creation, it is no coincidence that the number eight itself is the partner of the number three. Eight, then, belongs to the Wood element and is represented by the Liver in the body.

In *Qigong* practice, we work with the eight layers of the body: skin, muscles, tendons, fascia, blood vessels, bone, bone marrow, and blood. As we work to harmonize these eight layers and produce mutual cooperation among them, so too are we working with the eight trigrams of the body. *Qian* 乾 (Heaven) represents the head, as it is the highest part of the body. *Kun* 坤 (Earth) represents the belly, as it takes in nourishment and is the seat of the Spleen and Stomach. *Li* 離 (Fire) represents the eyes, as they are the windows of *Shen* (spirit). *Kan* 坎 (Water) represents the ears, as they are the orifices of the Kidney. *Zhen* 震 (Thunder) represents the feet, as they are the vehicle of life and the spiritual journey. *Xun* 巽 (Wind) represents the thighs, as they hold the *Yin* and *Yang* energy to balance the body. *Gen* 艮 (mountain) represents the hands, as they hold energy just as a mountain does. *Dui* 兌 (Lake) represents the mouth, as it makes speech and as a shaman chants for a joyful life. The number eight becomes a symbol of stability as these eight layers cooperate in cyclic generation.

5.10 *Jiugong* 九官/9 — Magic Square

In Chinese, the number nine is *Jiu* 九. In *Yijing* science, nine is the highest *Yang* number and is a symbol of change. Recall that the primary Five Element odd numbers one, three, and five are all *Yang*. Adding these three numbers together produces the highest *Yang* number, nine. According to *Yijing* principles, extreme *Yang* will transform to *Yin*, rendering the number nine a symbol of transformation. As the highest *Yang* number, nine represents transformation and change. Nine, then, becomes a symbol for deep understanding gained through that transformation. *Yang* is bright and moving, and it changes rapidly as opposed to *Yin*, which is contracted and therefore slower to change or transform. Much of our *Qigong* practice incorporates the number nine, as movements within the *Qigong* forms are often repeated nine times. This repetition centers on the highest *Yang* number and is quite effective for changing and refining the pattern of *Qi*.

Also of great significance are the nine palaces, or *Jiugong*, that illustrate the magic square. The magic square represents the eight directions of the *Bagua* (Eight Trigrams) with the addition of a ninth direction, that of center. The nine numbers are arranged in nine squares or palaces and placed so that addition of the numbers in any row or column adds up to fifteen. Fifteen is significant because it is produced by multiplying three (creation) and five (Five Elements). Each palace holding a number represents universal change. In ancient times, this magic square was used for divination.

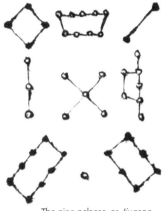

The nine palaces, or *Jiugong*, that illustrate the magic square.

In oracle bone writing, nine is illustrated with the shape of an arc or a half circle. It is similar to a stream winding along its course, as opposed to something traveling in a straight line. As water travels, it will "split" or change to accommodate a path and find the way, regardless of obstacles. This is the nature of nine as the highest *Yang* number reverting to *Yin*. The arc of the oracle bone is related to the symbol of the Uruborus, a snake/dragon biting itself in the tail. This symbol illustrates the infinite spiral of change and the concept of return—returning to our origin in the Dao. Our transformation and deep understanding of the number nine and the inevitability of its continual transformation and return is an illustration of infinity—the infinite and constant cycle of universal energy. The concept of infinity is further

Dragon painted on a pottery plate discovered in *Shanxi* 山西 Province; from 5,600 years ago.

iterated in the pronunciation of *Jiu*, which is the same tone and pronunciation for infinity in spoken Chinese. Thus, nine represents an immortal life. Nine is the partner of the number four and is related to the Metal organs of the Lung and Large Intestine in the body.

According to *Yijing* numerology, the number nine is the highest number of the fundamental number system. After nine, the numbering system returns to number one, the universal life force. Therefore, we can end our discussion of the number system here. However, there are two more important universal numbers that are related to daily life and spiritual cultivation. I want to expand our discussion to include these numbers: twelve and twenty-four.

5.11 *Shier Chen* 十二辰 /12 — Universal Transformation

Are you familiar with Chinese astrology? You may think of the twelve animals of the zodiac commonly printed on Chinese restaurant menus. In actuality, Chinese astrology is vastly more complicated than this. In Chinese astrology, the basic knowledge pertains to the Heavenly Stems and Earthly Branches. The number twelve is described as the twelve Earthly Branches. The branches are representative of the waxing and waning of the two primal energies of *Yin* and *Yang* throughout daily or yearly cycles.

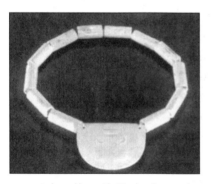

Jade necklace with 12 tube pieces and a pendant with a shaman face discovered in *Zhejiang* Province; from 5,600 years ago. The shaman face represents the Universal Way and the 12 tube pieces stand for the 十二辰 *Shier Chen.*

In Chinese, the number twelve is *Shier* 十二. It is a symbol for the universal clock, *Shier Chen* 十二辰, representing time and space. In Chinese cosmology, we certainly recognize the number twelve as contained in the twelve *Chen* 辰 (1 *Chen* equals 2 hours) in the day or the twelve months of the year. In Chinese medicine, the number twelve corresponds to the twelve meridian systems in the human body, or microcosm, which in turn correspond to the twelve months in the year and the twelve spiritual animals related to the zodiac. Twelve represents the energetic changes our bodies experience in a twelve-*Chen* day and in the twelve months of the year.

The Big Dipper is the heart of the celestial world, according to Chinese shamanic tradition. Ancient shamans noted 28 constellation patterns surrounding the Big Dipper. The Dipper rotated around these constellations, which remained fixed in the sky. For each constellation that the Dipper's handle pointed to, a change in energy was noted. The twelve animals of the zodiac originated from these constellations. Considered a trigger for natural phenomena occurring in the universe, the Big Dipper is responsible for unleashing natural disasters and for releasing disease. Accordingly, the Big Dipper has the function of governing the universal laws of the four seasons. It is believed to govern the general balance of *Yin* and *Yang* in the universe. The movement of the Dipper is patterned after the *Yin-Yang* movement of the Dao, which is the movement and Way of the Universe.

The chart below illustrates the aforementioned correspondences.

Universal Correspondences

Constellation	Earthly Branch	Animal	Direction/Space	Chen/Time
Xu	*Zi*	Rat	North	11 p.m. – 1 a.m.
Niu	*Chou*	Cow/Ox	North	1 a.m. – 3 a.m.
Wei	*Yin*	Tiger	East	3 a.m.– 5 a.m.
Fang	*Mao*	Rabbit	East	5 a.m. – 7 a.m.
Kang	*Chen*	Dragon	East	7 a.m. – 9 a.m.
Yi	*Si*	Snake	South	9 a.m. – 11 a.m.
Xing	*Wu*	Horse	South	11 a.m. – 1 p.m.
Gui	*Wei*	Sheep/Goat	South	1 p.m. – 3 p.m.
Zi	*Shen*	Monkey	West	3 p.m. – 5 p.m.
Mao	*You*	Rooster	West	5 p.m.– 7 p.m.
Lou	*Xu*	Dog	West	7 p.m. – 9 p.m.
Shi	*Hai*	Pig	North	9 p.m. – 11 p.m.

5.12 *Ershisi Jieqi* 二十四節气 /24 — Universal Rhythm

Please take a deep breath before we explore the number twenty-four. Can you tell which parts of your body are moving during your deep breath? Yes, the chest! More details, please? Yes, your ribs are moving in your chest. How many ribs are there? That's right. There are pairs of twelve ribs in the body, totaling 24 bilaterally. The number twenty-four is a secret number related to our breath and to the vital breath of the Dao.

In Chinese, the number twenty-four is *Ershisi*. It represents the rhythm of Universal *Qi*, i.e. *Ershisi Jieqi* 二十四節气. *Jie* 節 means segment, as in the segmented nodes on a piece of bamboo. When examining these segments on the bamboo plant, we can see a pattern or rhythm. Thus, *Jie* represents rhythm. In Chinese cosmology, every fifteen-day period is defined as *Qi*, and one year is divided into twenty-four segments of *Qi*, or *Jieqi* 節气. Every month begins a new section of *Jieqi*. Here, *Jie* means segment or rhythm and *Qi* is the breath of the universe. We come to understand *Jieqi* as the universal rhythm of *Qi* (breath).

Relating this to the microcosm of our bodies, we look to the Lung. Certainly, the Lung is in charge of breathing and therefore regulates the rhythm of *Qi*. In Chinese medicine, the function of the Lung is to control the rhythm of life, including the joints. The joints are known as *Guanjie* 関節 in Chinese. A literal translation would be gate node. Your joints, then, become a way to control the rhythms of your body. The Universal *Qi* is related to these joints. You may realize that many people with weak Lung function also have joint problems.

Chinese shamanism views the *Guanjie* (joints) as spiritual gates. There are twelve big joints in the body (hips, knees, ankles, shoulders, elbows, and wrists) making the total 24 bilaterally. Your spine, which is a spiritual channel, contains twenty-four vertebrae .

With regard to the tiger form you will learn in Part III *Laohu Gong* 老虎功 – Chinese Shamanic Tiger *Qigong* Form, there are twenty-four movements and all of them relate to the energy of the body. For each individual movement, there is a seasonal connection.

The spine is a spiritual channel. According to shamanic tradition, the spine has twenty-four vertebrae that are related to the *Ershisi Jieqi*.

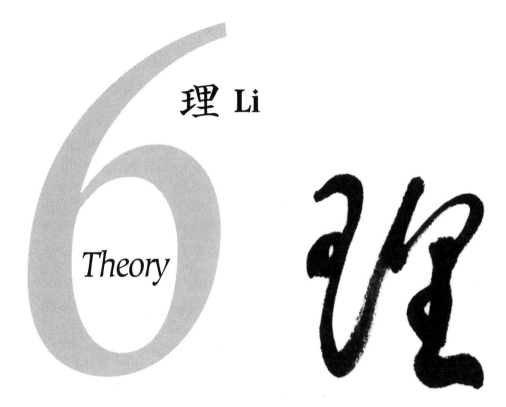

理 Li

6

Theory

6.1 *Qi* 气 — Vital Energy

6.1.1 Tea and *Qi*

Let us make a new pot of *Gongfu* tea before we talk about the *Qi* 气. Please take a deep breath and observe the new hot tea before you sip it. What do you notice? Yes, you can tell that steam or mist is rising from the surface of the teapot and tea cups. Do you smell the expanding fragrance of the tea? Yes, you are feeling refreshed from breathing in the steam and fragrance. In Chinese, both steam and fragrance are *Qi*. We call steam, vapor, or mist *Shui Qi* 水气 — water *Qi* — and fragrance *Xiang Qi* 香气 — perfume *Qi*.

The tea reminds us that *Qi* originated in ancient Chinese shamanism. Offering sacrifice (*Heng*) was an important way for ancient shamans to connect with higher-level spirits or with their ancestors. The mist or vapor rising from a sacrificial offering was understood to be a pattern of mystery, connection, and communication between Heaven and human beings. Thus, *Qi* is related to spirit and can be translated as spirit. The word *Qi* has been widely used in Chinese daily life for thousands of years to indicate different meanings. Let us take some time to learn more about it.

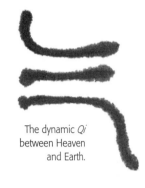

The dynamic *Qi* between Heaven and Earth.

The modern Chinese character stands for the universe full of *Qi*.

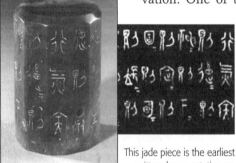

Fire is related to special spiritual cultivation. One of the fire radicals for Qi.

6.1.2 Five *Qi*

In *Qigong* theory, *Qi* is usually translated into English as breath or vital energy. The existence of Universal *Qi* is like a musical rhythm. Even if we can't see it, we can feel it in our bodies and in the environment through a deep heart/mind connection. Again, through the Chinese written character for *Qi*, we may learn more about it.

In Chinese, the word "*Qi* 气" can be written in five different writing patterns. Each pattern reveals a different symbolic meaning of this energetic *Qi*. I hope that understanding the different writing styles used to represent *Qi* will help us better understand *Qigong* and deepen our cultivation.

The oldest oracle bone style writing is similar to the Chinese character for the number three and has three horizontal lines 三 . The top and bottom lines were sometimes modified to picture the word *Qi*. It is an image of the dynamic *Qi* between Heaven and Earth. It looks like clouds and steam in, above, and below nature. This is the source of the modern Chinese character 气 (*Qi*). It stands for the universe full of *Qi*.

In my *Qigong* practice, I learned two other styles of writing *Qi* from my masters. Both of them have the radical *Huo* 火 (fire) at the bottom. Fire is a symbol of spirit in the Five Element principle. It is related to special spiritual cultivation. One of the fire radicals for *Qi* was found on a jade piece from 2,500 years ago. This character will not be found in any Chinese dictionary since its meaning is specific to Chinese shamanism. It means using fire for internal cultivation and shows that we need to use fire to refine our *Qi* to a better quality. A detailed *Qigong* technique was carved into this jade piece.

This jade piece is the earliest written documentation on *Qigong* that has been discovered so far.

The other fire radical for *Qi* 炁 has the radical *Wu* 无 (emptiness) on top and four dots at the bottom. These four dots together mean fire. This special character is used in internal cultivation as well. It means we need to empty our fire (postnatal mind) to move into a primordial state— no judgment, *Yin-Yang* in harmony.

The other fire radical for *Qi* has the radical *Wu* (emptiness) on top and four dots at the bottom.

The common Chinese character for *Qi* 氣 has the radical *Mi* 米 (rice) at the bottom. In ancient China, rice was one of the main foods. The character Mi indicates the eight directions of the universe and the energy moving systems. It represents the flowing *Qi* between Heaven and Earth. In the classical Chinese medicine cannon, *Huangdi Neijing*, only thirteen formulas were recorded. Rice soup was the first formula and its function was to strengthen energy. Why rice? Because it grows in a water place that holds high-quality *Yin* energy. It also needs good sunshine to gather *Yang* energy. Rice cannot grow everywhere in China. Rice is the symbol for nutrition. Water is the symbol for the pure *Yin* energy of the Earth; sun is the symbol for the pure *Yang* energy of Heaven.

The common Chinese character for *Qi* has the radical *Mi* (rice) at the bottom.

6.1.3 Manifesting *Qi*

Classical Chinese culture is a *Qi* 气 culture.[15] According to classical Chinese philosophy, *Qi* is the most basic and important material in the universe. *Qi* is the original energy of the universe and follows the laws of the cosmos as it cycles between tangible and intangible forms. "The pure *Qi* is *Qi* 气 [here meaning something like breath]; the turbid *Qi* is matter (*Zhi* 質)."[16] Its expression in the sky is found in the stars and in their movements. In the Earth, *Qi* is found in the mountains, oceans, air, and in all forms of life. For human beings, *Qi* manifests as the physical body and the processes of the mind. This animating energy connects us with the cosmos.

The concept of *Qi* pervades all aspects of Chinese culture and life sciences, including cosmology, philosophy, medicine, music, calligraphy, painting, martial arts, and *Qigong*. Daoist philosopher *Guanzi* 管子 (d. 645 BCE) described *Qi* in his *Neiye* 內業 (Inward Training) in the following poem:

凡物之精	*Speaking of the vital essence of beings,*
此則為生	*This is what gives them vitality.*
下生五谷	*It generates the five grains below.*
上為列星	*It becomes the arrayed stars above.*
流天地間	*When flowing between the Heavens and the Earth,*
謂之鬼神	*We refer to it as ghostly and spiritual.*
藏於胸中	*When stored within the human chest/heart,*
謂之聖人	*We call such beings sages.*[17]

6.2 *Qigong* 气功 — Spiritual Cultivation

6.2.1 *Qigong* and Its Root

Qigong 气功 is a traditional method of physical, mental, and *Shen* 神 (spiritual) cultivation. To learn the meanings of *Qi* and *Gong* is a way to deepen our understanding of *Qigong*. We learned the meaning of *Qi* while drinking the *Gongfu* tea, and the *Gongfu* tea will also help us learn the meaning of *Gong*.

Let us take a look at the Chinese character for *Gong*. This character contains the radical *Gong* 工 and the radical *Li* 力. *Gong* 工 means labor, project, skill, delicate, result, work, or worker. The original meaning of *Gong* 工 was a carpenter's square, which symbolized the universal law. We will discuss its symbolic meaning in the next section (6.3 *Wu* 巫—Chinese Shamanism). The second radical *Li* 力 means all one's best, force, power, effort, or strength. The *Han* Dynasty (206 BCE—200 CE) dictionary *Shouwen Jiezi* 説文解字 explains *Li* as "a pattern of tendons." Therefore, *Gong* 功 hints at the meaning that we should follow the correct way and work hard if we want to improve our skill. Following the correct way means finding and following the instruction of an illuminated teacher. Please remember, the illuminated teacher is not equivalent to the famous teacher. Be aware that some famous teachers are not authentic in their cultivation and are cheating their students.

Gong means work, exploit, skill, merit, or achievement, and it also means *Gongfu* 功夫. In Chinese, *Gongfu* means time and it also means a skill that develops over a long period of time and through strenuous effort. It is the same as our needing to take time to drink the *Gongfu* tea to learn the Way. Let us have another cup of *Gongfu* tea to review the details of *Gongfu* in Part I, 1.2.1 *Gongfu* and Tea.

From the perspective of ancient Chinese philosophy, the great Dao is composed of the interaction of one *Yin* and one *Yang* and its expression throughout the universe. Heaven represents the *Yang* component while Earth represents the *Yin* component.

The balance and union of these Heavenly *Yang* and Earthly *Yin* energies result in a peaceful and harmonious world. Likewise, imbalances in these energies can result in disharmony in the world, which can take the form of natural disasters such as earthquakes, storms, floods, and volcanic eruptions. As a part of this dynamic universe, human beings are also subject to the effects of these energies. By following and living by the balancing principles of the universe, it is possible to achieve harmony in the body. Through study and observation of this Universal Way, the ancient *Wu* created numerous methods to help people maintain/rebuild their body balancing systems in order to keep their bodies, minds, and spirits healthy. People have used these methods to improve their lives for thousands of years in China. Now, we call these modalities *Qigong*.

6.2.2 Forms of *Qigong*

Given the long history of *Qigong*, we may not fully understand its original function. Moreover, the benefits of *Qigong* practice have led many of us to focus only on the desired results rather than on the deep roots of *Qigong*. Yes, it is true that we can do Eye *Qigong* to improve eyesight, or Strengthening *Qigong* to eliminate cancer, or other *Qigong* forms to treat particular health concerns. However, in my personal experience, mastering the roots of *Qigong* practice is a better way to enhance our cultivation.

Qigong practice takes many forms: sitting meditation, breathwork, regulation of mental focus and emotions, visualization, mudras, mantras, and movement— including *Taijiquan* and other martial arts. The proper use of herbal supplements and food choices can also be associated with *Qigong*. Cultivation of the classical arts, such as calligraphy and music, is considered a form of *Qigong* when conducted in a mindful manner. In any case, all the different forms have the same three keys, or three alignments: regulating the posture, regulating the breath, and regulating the mind. *Qigong* facilitates the development of a deeper relationship with *Qi*. This relationship helps the practitioner understand the laws of the universe and how they influence human life. In its true form, *Qigong* is a practice for cultivating knowledge and a main method for moving into *Tian Ren He Yi* 天人合一 (the union of the human being and the universe).

6.2.3 The Five Essential Techniques of *Qigong* Practice

Although there are thousands of different *Qigong* forms in modern times, there are five essential techniques of *Qigong* practice in traditional forms.[18] Whenever you practice any of the *Qigong* forms, you need to use all of these techniques in your daily practice. Otherwise, the *Qigong* practice will be incomplete. These five essential techniques are regulating the heart/mind, regulating the breath, regulating the posture, regulating the diet, and regulating the sleep

Regulating the heart/mind is a technique to calm your mind and tune your consciousness into tranquility. It is the way to refine your *Shen* 神 (spiritual energy) and improve your health on the spiritual level. In Chinese shamanism, a healthy physical body always holds its spiritual body. A person will become ill if the spiritual body separates from the physical body. For instance, a person who tries hard to find a job and doesn't succeed for a long time will find that the digestion function may become imbalanced because the Will (Spleen spirit) will have deserted the spleen and caused this problem. Consequently, ancient Chinese shamans invented many modalities to help people retain the spiritual body in the physical body and transform the spiritual body into a high-level cultivation state: Enlightenment. In Chinese shamanic *Qigong* practice, we use different visualization techniques to bring the mind back to the physical body to release illness and maintain well-being.

Regulating the breath is a way to help you to relax and achieve tranquility. It is a way to strengthen your life force and harmonize the flowing *Qi* and blood. It is an important way to unite the physical body and spiritual body. The four patterns of the breath are: *Feng* 风 (wind), *Chuan* 喘 (wheeze), *Qi* 气 (air), and *Xi* 息 (grow). *Feng* means there is noise during breathing. *Chuan* means there is blockage in the breath, even without noise during breathing. *Qi* means the breath is heavy, even without noise or blockage during breathing. These three breathing patterns are not harmonious. The fourth one, *Xi*, is the harmonious and balancing breathing pattern. *Xi* means the breath is smooth without blockage, soft and constant without noise. A *Qigong* practitioner is able to calm the mind and allow the consciousness to stay in a peaceful, harmonious, tranquil state through practicing *Xi*. In Chinese shamanic traditions, we apply mantras to elevate the breath to the *Xi* level.

Regulating the posture is a way to strengthen your physical body. It is a way to help circulate the *Qi* and blood and to relax the mind through correct posture. The four postures in *Qigong* practice are: standing, sitting, walking, and lying down. You can practice *Qigong* anywhere and anytime in your daily life with these four postures. In shamanic tradition, we call these four postures *Siweiyi* 四威仪 (four sincere rituals). If we observe an enlightened being on a superficial level, that being may appear to act like a normal person, but the enlightened being actually lives with the Dao in every moment. In *Qigong* practice, we should train ourselves to stay in the Dao in our daily lives with these *Siweiyi*.

Regulating the diet is a way to nourish your body and *Shen* 神 with proper food. We need to eat everyday. We will get weak if we do not eat for many days. However, the *Huandi Neijing* indicates that we will get sick if we eat too much rich food. Modern science has proved that many diseases are related to improper eating or food problems. The ancient Chinese shamans understood that food was medicine (See Part I, 1.5.2 The Dao of Food). We should eat healthy food that is suitable for us. As *Qigong* practitioners, we should learn the natural diet rhythm and follow the teaching of *Song* Dynasty *Taiji* ancestral master *Zhang Sanfeng* (born 1247 AD): "Please eat when you feel hungry."[19] In other words, do not overeat and do not starve yourself; these are the right standards for you. Of course, you can shift yourself into a *Bigu* 辟谷 (avoid food) state and go without any food for a certain period of time after you have practiced *Qigong* correctly for a long time.

Regulating the sleep is a way to strengthen your health and refine your *Shen* 神 during sleep. You spend almost one-third of your life sleeping. A good quality sleep will recharge you and make your *Shen* 神 strong. A poor quality sleep will make you feel exhausted and grumpy. To help our students improve the quality of sleep, we teach a sleeping *Qigong* form. When your energy gets strong, you will need less sleep than normal but do not force yourself to reduce the sleeping time. "You should go to sleep when you feel sleepy."[20] You may do meditation for hours in your sleeping time to replace regular sleep. My master, *Yu Wencai* 于文才, was an outstanding example of this practice. He did sitting meditation during his sleeping time without lying down for over sixty years.

6.2.4 The Tranquility of *Qigong* Practice

Many *Qigong* friends have told me that their minds always wander from the present at the beginning of their *Qigong* training. Some friends have given up their *Qigong* practice because they could not calm down during *Qigong*. Actually, an uneven feeling is a normal phenomenon of *Qigong* processing. It is not necessary to try to force yourself to calm down during your practice. The ancient shamans designed different *Qigong* techniques to help people become tranquil. The feelings of stillness, peacefulness, and tranquility are the results of *Qigong* practice. Holding the tranquility state is a way to awaken your *Shen* 神 (spirit). For instance, in classical Chinese medicine, practitioners in a deep state of tranquility may feel or see how the meridian systems are working in their bodies or may be able to tell how an herb is connecting with the different organ systems.

Again, tranquility is a result of *Qigong* practice rather than a requirement. In the *Daodejing*, a book about *Qigong* practice and spiritual cultivation, *Laozi* taught all of the *Qigong* principles and techniques. We can find this tranquility of *Qigong* processing in the following passage from his book:

孔德之容	*The Hole (Dantian) functions as a container,*
唯道是從	*It follows only the Dao.*
道之為物	*Everything comes from the Dao.*
惟恍惟惚	*It is elusive, evasive.*
惚兮恍	*Evasive, elusive,*
其中有象	*Yet latent within it are patterns.*
恍兮惚	*Elusive, evasive,*
其中有物	*Yet latent within it are objects.*
窈兮冥	*Dark and dim,*
其中有精	*Yet latent within it is the Jing (life force).*
其精甚真	*The Jing being very true,*
其中有信	*Latent within it is Xin (trust, integrity, evidence).*[21]

We will achieve an enlightened nature through the state of tranquility. The original function of *Qigong* was to model a way of life as well as to reach a state of Enlightenment. Exploring the roots of *Qigong*—*Wu*, Chinese shamanism—may help us understand and deepen our *Qigong* practice.

6.3 *Wu* 巫 — Chinese Shamanism

When I was a child in China, I was curious about the way that local *Wu* (Chinese shaman) gave treatments to patients. How could an acupuncture needle release the pain when the *Wu* put it in a suffering patient's body? How could the *Wu's* chanting help patients recover from sickness? I came to understand more about Chinese medicine when I grew up, of course, but I did get answers to my questions in childhood. Still, I had more questions such as: What are meridians? What is an acupuncture point? Where did this knowledge come from? How did it come to us? Through years and years of *Qigong* practice, I got the answers to all of these questions. I understood that ancient *Wu* (Chinese Shamanism) is the root of Chinese culture, which includes *Qigong* and classical Chinese medicine. I felt that learning *Wu* could help me better understand Chinese medicine because *Wu* is more of a practical or experiential knowledge than learning through words alone. Words, however, may inspire and guide us to deepen our cultivation and practice. For this reason I want to share some *Wu* information through my writing.

6.3.1 The Emperor as *Wu* 巫 (Shaman)

Classical Chinese culture is based on *Wu*, which predates both Daoist and Confucian culture. The ancient Chinese emperors were *Wu*, and through the ancient Chinese classics, we can understand the role of the *Wu*. In fact, many of the classics are named after great emperors or sages.

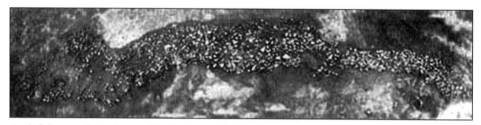

Seashell dragon sculpture discovered in *Liaoning* 遼寧 Province in 1994; from 8,000 years ago.

Artifacts from the *Peiligang* 裴李崗, *Hongshan* 紅山, and *Yangshao* 仰韶 cultures (5,000—3,000 BCE) show that *Wu* culture has existed for more than 8,000 years of Chinese history. The levels of knowledge and mastery over the material and non-material elements of the world achieved by the *Wu* were indeed profound and were highly regarded throughout most of ancient China. All of the legendary sages and cultural heroes of China's proto-historical past possessed the remarkable superhuman attributes of the *Wu*. The treasures of unearthed oracle bones and other artifacts reveal that the *Wu* were most esteemed during China's Three Dynasties (*Xia* 夏, *Shang* 商, and *Zhou* 周) period (2100—256 BCE), which is when they achieved their greatest prominence. In his research into the *Shang Wu*, archaeological scholar *Chen Mengjia* identifies the king as a shaman:

Head of a female shaman from a clay statue; from about 6,000 years ago.

Some of the oracle bone inscriptions (used in ritual divination) state that the "king divined" or that "the king inquired in connection with wind"—or rainstorms, rituals, conquests, or hunts. Also prevalent were statements such as "the king made the prognostication that ...," pertaining to weather, the border regions, or misfortunes and diseases; the only prognosticator ever recorded in the oracle bone inscriptions was the king...In addition, inscriptions describing the king dancing to pray for rain and the king prognosticating about a dream are numerous. All of these were activities of both king and shaman, which indicate in effect that the king was a shaman.[22]

6.3.2 The Nature of *Wu* 巫

The Chinese character *Wu* can be used as a noun or an adjective and it can also be translated as shaman, shamanism, or shamanic. As discussed in my article, "Drumming and Dancing: Feeling the Rhythm of *Qigong*, Calligraphy, and *Wu* (Shamanism),"[23] the Chinese character *Wu* is commonly translated as shaman—a somewhat incomplete interpretation. The word shaman comes from the Tungusu-Manchurian language. The practice of a *Wu* only distantly resembles that of current day shamans, who travel in "alternative realities" as part of their religious practices. They are mostly located in Siberia and are very aggressive. In trance, but still in full possession of their faculties, these shamans may climb the World Tree to reach the "Heaven of the Ancestors" or descend to an underworld in search of lost or trapped souls. They undergo difficult and painful initiations, including ritual death and rebirth. In contrast, the *Wu* referred to by the Chinese character is much more of a spirit-medium. Through natural ability, training, and ritual preparation, the *Wu* can summon the bright spirits. These spirits inhabit and speak through the *Wu's* body.[24]

Shamans specialize in ritual and possess unique powers that enable them to act as intermediaries between humans and the shadowy world of spirits and the supernatural. However, the ancient *Wu* were not similar to modern-day shamans and they were different from the modern concept of *Wu*. Today's *Wu* may channel transmissions from spirit bodies without being able to recall the communication. In ancient China, the *Wu* were omniscient and they governed the country in addition to aiding others in transcending the physical plane. They were also able to function as doctors and taught disease prevention. Their keen observation of and close relationship with the universe enabled them to avert natural disasters. Indeed, the *Wu* possessed *Shenming* 神明 (literally "Spiritual Clarity" or "Spiritual Brightness"): Spiritual Enlightenment and a deep understanding of the Universal Way. The *Wu* were enlightened beings who embodied *Tian Ren He Yi* 天人合一 . Through this ritual connection with Heaven, they sustained both *Yin* and *Yang*—stillness and movement.[25]

6.3.3 The Function of *Wu* 巫

Wu specialists could call souls and their spirits, and they could travel to the four directions. They were magical healers, exorcists, prophets, fortunetellers, rainmakers, and dream interpreters who used music and dance in their rites. The *Shang Wu* 商巫 specialists correspond to what we think of as shamans, although Westerners typically lump many types of Chinese religious specialists together and call all of them shamans.

The Chinese character *Wu* 巫 carries a great deal of meaning. The common character for *Wu* is written as 巫 , which contains the radical *Gong* 工 (work) and *Ren* 人 (person). It is an image of two people working together or two shamans doing their ritual dance. The syllable *Wu*, written and intoned differently, also means dancing. It is no coincidence that dancing connects the *Wu* to the universe and helps develop their *Shenming*. According to *Xici* 繫辭 , as written in one of the Ten Wings of the *Yijing*,[26] we can achieve a full understanding of our own *Shen* and communicate with high-level beings through dancing and drumming. Dancing and drumming are methods to help us understand the *Shen*. This is illustrated on ancient pottery from more than five thousand years ago. Even the shamans of today use the ritual of dancing to facilitate universal connections such as bringing rain to dry farmland. The ancient *Wu* were able to elevate their spirits to become one with all other spirits.

Similarly, in the *Shang* oracle bones, the Chinese character *Wu* is written with two of the same radicals for *Gong* 工, which means work. Literally, this radical stands for a carpenter's square, a tool used for making squares (*Fang* 方). This is significant because in ancient *Wu* time, *Gong*, a carpenter's square, was the universal measurement tool, and it stood for order and correct behavior or

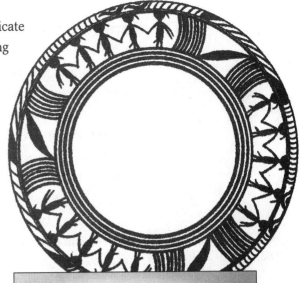

Pottery bowl discovered in *Gansu* Province has three groups of shamans dancing around the edge of the bowl; from about 5,600 years ago. The numbers three and five represent the Universal Way.

the law of nature. *Fuxi*, the original ancestor of the human being according to a Chinese creation myth, holds the *Gong* as shown in an ancient scroll. In the *Huangdi Neijing* (Classic of Medicine), *Gong* 工 means doctor. Ancient Chinese medicine doctors were no different from the *Wu*. They had the ability to help

Stone carving of *Fuxi*, from the early *Han* Dynasty.

people because they understood The Way of the Universe and the truth of life. Therefore, the original function of *Wu* was to connect with universal energy (or living in the Dao) and to pass this universal knowledge on to others.

6.3.4 The Root of Chinese Medicine

The character *Wu* depicts *Sifang* 四方 —four directions or four quadrants (squares). *Sifang* can be translated as the four cardinal directions—North, South, East, and West. This is the pattern that the ancient *Wu* applied to the center of their bodies as "high-tech" equipment to communicate with the other four directions, and it was through this practice that they understood the Universal Way. This practice is called *Zhongdao* 中道 (Central Way) in Chinese. In this *Wu* tradition, the body is the central direction and is coordinated with the other four directions. Therefore, *Sifang* (four directions) includes the fifth direction—the center. These five directions in *Fang* are equal to the Five Elements in Chinese philosophy. My guess is that the Five Element philosophy originated in this *Wu* function.

Ancient Chinese doctors had the same ability as the *Wu*. *Zhongyi* 中醫 —(Chinese medicine) can be translated as central way of medicine. Classical Chinese medicine (CCM) and Chinese shamanism are also widely considered to have origi- nated from the same source (*Wu Yi Tong Yuan* 巫醫同源). Many ancient Chinese documents verify that doctors were indeed shamans.[27] Confucius indicates in Chapter 13 of *Lunyu* 論語 (Analects) that: "A person should not be a *Wu* (shaman) and/or doctor if that person is without constancy [dedicated to the practice]." CCM, which merged with Daoism and Confucianism, is thoroughly based on the *Yijing* (*I Ching* or Book of Changes), the divination book of the ancient *Wu*. The *Tang* Dynasty sage and Medical King *Sun Simiao* 孫思邈 stated, "Nobody qualifies to be a master physician without knowledge of the Science of the *Yijing*."[28]

Therefore, *Wu* (Chinese shamanism) is the source of all classical Chinese tra- ditions. Through their ability to communicate with nature, the ancient *Wu*—the enlightened beings—created the philosophy of the ancient Chinese cosmos that affected the whole of Chinese history and culture—and this cosmology became the fundamental elements of *Qigong* and Classical Chinese medicine.

6.4 *Fang* 方 — Cosmos

6.4.1 Space and Time

As commonly understood, *Fang* 方 means directions, method, place, square, or way. In Chinese oracle style writing, the character *Fang* is similar to the *Wu* in that it looks like a person holding the *Wu* ruler and using it as a tool to measure the universe. *Fang* is the way that the ancient *Wu* applied this tool to understand the universe. *Fang* also represents the cosmos. If you have the right tool, you will understand the Way. In traditional Chinese philosophy, we can use *Fang* to represent space and time. Actually, the ancient Chinese concept of the universe is related to space and time. The Chinese name for the universe is *Yuzhou* 宇宙. In the *Han* Dynasty Daoist cosmology book *Huainanzi* 淮南子, the definition of *Yu* is up, down, or four directions (front, back, left, and right), and the definition of *Zhou* is past, present, and future.[29]

The character *Wu* depicts *Sifang* —four directions or four quadrants (squares).

In Chinese medicine, *Fang* stands for formula as well. Making a formula is *Zufang* 組方, which originally meant to organize different directions of the universal *Qi* or different location or time energies in the formula through the herbs to heal the body. It hints that the ancient *Wu* understood through their bodies (the center) that different herbal formulas had different Universal *Qi* associated with different directions and different place and time periods. A *Wu*/doctor prepared a formula to reorganize the patient's body (microcosm).

In Chinese oracle style writing, the character *Fang* is similar to the *Wu* in that it looks like a person holding the *Wu* ruler and using it as a tool to measure the universe.

Ancient *Wu* created their cosmology through the *Fang*. In the *Wu* cosmological perspective, the universe—*Fang*—is constructed of three layers in space and time. In space, the layers are: upper layer, *Tian* (Heaven); lower layer, *Di* (Earth); and middle layer, *Ren* (Humanity). In time, the layers are past, present, and future. Human beings are a microcosm reflecting this macrocosm. Human beings are also constructed of three layers: *Jing* (essence), *Qi* (vital energy or life force), and *Shen* (spirit). Each layer contains its own *Fang*. Therefore, in *Yijing* numerology science, the numbers three and five embody the Way of the Universe. We discussed the number five in Part II, 5.6 (*Wuxing* 五行 /5 — Five Elements). Now, let us take a look at a mysterious ancient painting to learn more about the three layers.

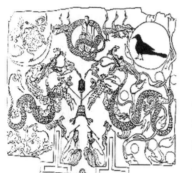

6.4.2 A Mysterious Painting

A silk painting on this *Feiyi* 非衣 displays an understanding of this ancient *Wu* cosmos as it was conceived in the *Han* Dynasty and in earlier times. *Feiyi*, literally meaning flying cloth, is a silk funerary banner. This *Feiyi*, (discovered in 1972 in *Mawangdui* Tomb Number One, which was unearthed near modern-day Changsha, *Hunan* Province) is a pictorial memorial of a deceased person. Dated to the 180's BCE, it resembles an article of clothing and presents the human body on a scale larger than its mere physical form. It is pictured as a microcosm of the universe.

This painting contains both natural and supernatural elements. Many of these elements refer to the *Shang* Dynasty creation myths and that era's particular vision of the afterworld. The painting is structured along a vertical axis of three divisions: an upper Heavenly mythical celestial realm, a middle realm of human-centered activity, and a lower Earthly murky subterranean netherworld. The landscape in the upper section of the painting has various details: a solitary sun containing the profile of a black bird and the partial phase of a moon containing a toad, a tree with the other eight suns[31] or planets of the solar system, and a person in the center of a coiled dragon or snake tail between the sun and moon.

These are all references to earlier Chinese cosmological myths. In the middle layer of the painting is a portrayal of the daily life of a noblewoman with her people. In the lower scene at the bottom of the painting is a depiction of a watery underworld, populated with strange and sometimes grotesque aquatic creatures. On each side of the painting, a dragon links the three layers of the universe. These two dragons symbolize the unity of the mundane or physical world, the

Silk painting of the shamanic cosmos on a funerary banner; from about 2,200 years ago.[30]

mythical realms of Heaven, and the underworld while producing a dynamic pattern that is smooth, embracing, free-flowing, and balanced. This movement is alive and vital, pulsing, sinuous, and seemingly perpetual and harmonious. This painting evokes the feeling that the time-bound and the timeless are linked, that mundane reality and the super-mundane landscape of myth are in some way connected, the natural and supernatural joined.[32]

This painting is also a symbol of the human microcosm, as I mentioned earlier. The upper part of the painting symbolizes the head and *Shen* (spirit); the middle part stands for the organ system and *Qi* (life force and breath), and the lower part of the painting represents the lower body and the *Jing* (essence). The dragons are a symbol for the *Qi* (vital energy) that unites the whole body. A free dragon symbolizes the pattern of free-flowing *Qi* in a living body. For example, the person in the middle of the coiled tail in the painting reminds me of the story of the giant *Pangu* 盘古. *Pan* means "coil" and *Gu* means "ancient." *Pangu* can be interpreted as "coiling the origin." Please read the Chinese creation myth of *Pangu* in Part II, 4.2.2 (*Pangu* 盘古 — The Giant).

6.4.3 *Wu* Cosmos and *Qigong*

The roots of classical style *Qigong* originate in the ancient world of *Wu*. A good way to understand our *Qigong* practice is to learn about the ancient *Wu* and their practices. The *Wu* cosmos is the basis of Chinese cosmology. The universe is constructed of Heaven, Humanity, and Earth; this is the pattern of a person in terms of ancient Chinese *Wu*. In traditional *Qigong* practice, regardless of the style, practitioners always work with these three layers of the body. Please see the chart below for details:

Chinese Cosmology					
Heaven	Head	*Shen*	Spirit	Regulate the heart	Visualization
Humanity	Organ systems	*Qi*	Life force	Regulate the breath	Breath
Earth	Limbs	*Jing*	Essence	Regulate the posture	Body

As the microcosm of the universal macrocosm, the body contains all the information of the universe and communicates with the universe all the time. We can deepen our *Qigong* practice through the study of *Wu* and, at the same time, become more aware of our bodies while developing the relationship between the human being and nature.

6.5 *Shengsi* 生死 — Birth and Death

Sheng 生 means birth, alive, vital energy, flex, life, or grow. *Si* 死 means stiff, stagnant, or death. In ancient Chinese shamanism, one of the most important concepts is respect for the *Sheng*, or in other words, respect for all living beings. The human being is the most precious of all living beings; therefore, the ancient shamans developed numerous techniques to preserve human beings. In modern times, we call these techniques *Qigong*. *Qigong* is a way to learn about the *Sheng*.

6.5.1 Past, Present, and Future

From the shamanic perspective, to learn about the *Sheng* we must understand the *Si* (death) because once we are born, we face death. It is the same for all beings. Birth is the beginning of death. The ancient shamans didn't think that death was the end of life. They thought of death as the gateway to new life. In shamanic cosmology, the past, present, and future are all one; they are non-separate, so all beings exist in concurrent past, present, and future lives. The important part to remember is that the present life must be treasured because it is the result of the past life, and the future life will be the result of this present life. All of our lives are connected.

People are often curious about their past lives and want to know what their past lives were like. However, this is not important because the past is past. If you really want to know about your past life, study your present life because it is a reflection of your past lives. Actually, in the present life, all of us experience our past and future lives.

Many people are afraid of what the future will bring. They are afraid they will get sick and they are afraid of death, but they don't really think about what they should do for their health now in the present. They don't really treasure the moment and they may be wasting their vital energy by ignoring the present. Then, when death is coming, they fear it. In this moment, they experience the future but do not realize it. If they truly understand that the future and this moment are connected, they can cultivate in a high spiritual way and will understand what will happen in their future and not have a fear of death. They can enjoy each moment and when death comes, they can enjoy that moment, too, because that is the time for shifting the spirit into another life pattern. Death is a transcendent moment for an enlightened being to cherish the new life that is coming.

6.5.2 The Life Cycle

Ancient Chinese shamans understood that life is part of nature and that the life cycle is the same as the cycle of nature. The human life cycle can be compared with the four seasons of the year: spring corresponds to the life stage of zero to 20 years old; summer is from 20-40 years old, autumn is from 40-60 years old. Winter starts after 60 years old. Of course, an enlightened being is one who has jumped out of this cycle since high-level spiritual practitioners may transfer the physical body back to the spring stage.

The first stage of life, from birth to young adult, is the spring season. As we can see in nature, new life is emerging and growing in the spring. Farmers need to take good care of their land during this season. They need to plow and fertilize the land, sow the seeds, and feed, water, and fertilize their plants. Similar to this pattern in nature, Chinese shamans regard a new baby as a new "life tree" in the world. Parents need to take good care of their babies on the physical and spiritual levels. During the baby-to-young-adult stage, a person is not only growing physically very quickly but is also learning very quickly. A person should study and get a good education during this time period because this is the best time for learning. People at this life stage have the best memories and the ability to easily absorb knowledge.

The second stage of life, from young adult to middle-age, is the summer season. In the summer, the plants grow and we can see their features clearly. All living beings reach their peak life energy in the summer season. The *Yijing* tells us that the Ten Thousand Things are coming together in this season. This means that natural life energy reaches its peak. In summer, *Yang* energy is the strongest in nature and in human beings. It is the time when a person's physical body has finished growing, education has been completed, and knowledge in a specific field has been developed. Therefore, the person can start achieving lifetime goals. Confucius said, "A person in his thirties should be established." This means people in business should have their own companies and people in academia should have their own theories in their fields of expertise.

The third stage of life, from middle-age to older-age, is autumn season, the harvest time. People in this time period should enjoy their lives, enjoy the harvest rather than live in fear. Maturity (the fifties) is autumn time. In this stage, people are living more in the spiritual layer and their wisdom is growing into maturity—like the harvest. Confucius said, "In your fifties, you should understand your Heavenly life (karmic life)." If you understand your life, you won't worry about your life and death.

6.5.3 An Eternal Life

A life is like a tree or a plant. In the death period of winter, a tree holds its life energy in its roots and waits for spring to come. Seeds embrace their life energy and wait to sprout. This is the death time and the prenatal time, a time of transition. Winter is preparing for spring. It is the time for selecting and storing the best quality seeds for the next year. Once spring comes, the seeds can be planted. This is like the prenatal time before the egg and sperm come together. In the old tradition, parents cultivated before the father and mother had a baby; they needed to prepare for the new life coming. The old wisdom traditions specified a lot of techniques for preparing the womb to receive the seed. In the moment that the sperm and egg combine, the universal energy and ancestral energy combine and new life is created. This time period is equal to the transition time between winter and spring. Winter is the death time, and death is the processing period for the new birth.

Life is eternal. The significance of eternal life is like growing plants. If we take good care of the seeds in the winter and store them carefully, life comes back more strongly in the spring and a better harvest will result. So, in the present, we need to treasure our lives and take care of our bodies in the physical and spiritual layers. Then when death comes, we will not be afraid because we will have a deeper understanding of the whole process or pattern of birth and death.

In the Chinese shamanic tradition, people don't worry about death and are calm in facing death. In my memory, my grandmother was in her sixties when she prepared her coffin. She chose all the materials by herself to get ready for death. This is a very old tradition. In her case, death did not come for more than twenty years, but she still got ready for it. She passed away in her nineties. Believe you have your eternal life and then you will treasure your current life.

6.6 Jing 精 — Essence

Jing means best, essence, or subtle. The Chinese character for *Jing* is composed of the radical for rice and the radical for the color green. The original meaning of *Jing* was the best quality rice. In ancient Chinese tradition, rice holds the best Universal *Qi*. The radical for green is also symbolic of life energy. Ancient shamans used rice as an important remedy to treat patients. When a patient was very weak, the shaman would use rice soup to tonify the patient's vital energy and help the patient recover. As I mentioned before, the first of the Chinese Medicine Classics, *Huangdi Neijing*, has only thirteen formulas and rice soup is the first formula.

In the shamanic tradition, *Jing* also represents the physical body. Different parts of the body have different qualities of *Jing*. The ancient shamans also used the word *Jing* to mean body fluid because the body is a container for water in the same way the Earth is a container for water. In the Five Organ System, the Water organ is the Kidney. In a specific way, *Jing* also represents the Kidney essence. From the *Qigong* perspective, all the body fluids, especially the sexual fluids, can be considered *Jing*. This includes the blood, saliva, and all other material body fluids.

As we discussed in Part II, 6.4 *Fang* 方 — Cosmos, the body has three layers, *Jing*, *Qi*, and *Shen*. *Jing* represents the physical layer and is the root of the *Qi* body and the *Shen* (spirit) body. A person with strong *Jing* will have a strong *Qi* body and a strong *Shen* body. In Chinese, we have a saying: *Jing Zu Shen Wang* 精足神旺. It means you will have strong spiritual energy if you have an abundance of *Jing*.

In *Qigong* practice, the first important step is *Lianye* 煉液, which literally means refine the water. Actually, this step is about how to strengthen the physical body to improve health and to transform the physical body into a *Qi* body. In practice, we treasure the *Jing* and take care not to waste it. This includes swallowing the saliva, which in *Qigong* is referred to as *Changshengshui* 長生水 —long-life water. Swallowing the saliva down to the *Dantian* helps nourish the body.

A person's *Jing* is regular, non-refined water if it has not been transformed through *Lianye*. In this case, it will still be in a low-level water state. "Water always finds the lowest position." Refinement is what must occur in order for it to reach the *Shen* from this low state. By cooking the water over fire, we create steam and vapor; this is how *Jing* is transformed into *Qi*. The next step is *Shenghua* 升華 (transcendence) whereby the transformed water is brought from a low position to a high position."[33]

Laozi said that ruling a great country is like cooking a small fish.[34] In *Qigong* practice, we must cook. In other words, the visible physical liquid must be transformed through internal alchemy (the "cooking") to invisible *Qi* and then to *Shen*.[35]

6.7 *Shen* 神 — Spirit

Shen means spirit and it also means great, marvelous, or elegant. *Shen* represents the spiritual energy of the Heart. In oracle bone style writing, *Shen* is the pattern of lightning. Breaking the darkness with thunder, a pattern of lightning, was considered an omen from Heaven in ancient Chinese shamanism. The ancient *Wu* understood the Universal Way through observing and studying the patterns in nature. The ancient *Wu* used *Shen* as a symbol for spirit, divinity, deity, infinite, omniscience, and Enlightenment. *Shen* also means stretch because natural lightning stretches between Heaven and Earth. In spiritual cultivation, we use many physical stretching techniques to open our spiritual gates to connect with our own spirits and with high-level spiritual energy. The shaman sees that each part of the body has its own spirit residing in each physical part. In spiritual cultivation, the important processing step is to call the spiritual body back to the physical body. This is the reuniting of the physical body (*Yin*) and the spiritual body (*Yang*). This is the Way of the Dao. The *Yijing* gives the definition of Dao as one *Yin* and one *Yang* combined.

The physical body is made up of three layers. The upper layer is the head and represents Heaven and *Shen* (Spirit). The lower body includes the legs and feet and represents the Earth and *Jing* (essence). The middle layer, between Heaven and Earth, is the Five Organ System and represents the human being and *Qi* (vital energy). Therefore, ancient shamans used the five organ systems to discuss the health of the whole body.

In the five physical organ systems, each organ system has its own particular kind of spiritual body. Let us take a look at the five spiritual energies of these five organ systems before we go into the details. The Liver system spiritual energy is *Hun* 魂 —*Yang* Soul. The Lung system spiritual energy is *Po* 魄—*Yin* Soul. The Spleen system spiritual energy is *Yi* 意 —Will. The Kidney system spiritual energy is *Zhi* 志 —Memory. The Heart system spiritual energy is *Shen* 神 —Spirit. We will use these five spiritual bodies as an example for discussing the physical and spiritual connections in the body. Let's learn another Chinese character, *Ling* 靈—Soul, before we move on.

6.7.1 *Ling* 靈 — Soul

Ling is usually translated into English as soul. Additional meanings include inspiration, transformation, shaman, or spirit. The Chinese character *Ling* is composed of three parts. The upper part is the radical *Yu* 雨 for rain. The middle part is composed of three of the same radical, *Kou* 口 for mouth. The lower part is the radical *Wu* 巫 for shaman. This character is an image of a shaman using the mouth to repeat a mantra to bring rain. The shaman has the ability to make the rain happen. This is the result of using spiritual energy to make the connection between the human being and nature, which was the original function of *Ling*. In the ancient *Chu* 楚 State (approximately 1100—223 BCE) in China, shamans had the ability to use their spiritual energy to help people, so people addressed them as *Ling*. Therefore, *Ling* also means shaman.

Another meaning of *Ling* is verify. For example, the shaman makes the rain happen to verify his authenticity and we call this result *Ling*. A shaman who cannot make the rain fall is described as being "without *Ling*" or without verification. In spiritual cultivation, we need to work with our soul energy to verify our spiritual experiences. This kind of spiritual cultivation we call inner verification because only through the body can we understand the spiritual journey. No words can fully describe the inner experience. Once a person has had the true experience of spiritual cultivation, we will say the person has *Ling*. When the spiritual body and physical body combine and the spiritual body is able to guide the physical body to function well, we also call this *Ling*. *Ling* is the function of the spirit.

6.7.2 *Hun* 魂 — *Yang* Soul

The spiritual energy of the Liver system is *Hun* 魂 — *Yang* Soul. The Chinese character *Hun* is composed of the radical *Yun* 云 for cloud and the radical *Gui* 鬼 for ghost. In Chinese, ghost means condense or return. When ordinary people die, their spiritual energy returns to the Earth. This returning of spiritual energy we call *Gui* 鬼, ghost. In contrast, when people who are high-level spiritual beings die, their spiritual energy transcends into Heaven. This spiritual energy we call *Shen*. The radical *Yun* 云 for cloud is a symbol for ascending. Therefore, *Hun* is the Liver spiritual energy as the wandering soul. The function of *Hun* is to make the energy of the Liver ascend. The ancient shamans saw that this spiritual energy in the body is the same as the nature spirit of the sun. This spiritual energy of the sun is also called *Hun*. Since the sun rises from the East every morning, the Liver system is associated with the eastern direction and the Wood element. Morning is the Liver system activity time.

When a person's *Hun* energy decreases, the lower level will affect the Liver function and the person may have depression, stress, anger, and associated symptoms because the Liver ascending function has a problem. Once the *Hun* separates from the Liver, it will be very dangerous for the person. The person may become insane, or the immune system will be very low, or the person may be facing death. People with strong *Hun* energy combined with the Liver system are likely to have strong life energy and be doing well.

6.7.3 *Po* 魄 — *Yin* Soul

The spiritual energy of the Lung system is *Po* 魄 — *Yin* Soul. The Chinese character *Po* is composed of the radical *Bai* 白 for white and the radical *Gui* 鬼 for ghost. We discussed the ghost in the *Hun* section. Now we will discuss the radical *Bai* 白 for white. According to the Five Element principle, white belongs to the Metal element and includes all of the minerals and the metal materials. The ancient shamans saw that when the white quality descended, it was an indication of death. In Chinese tradition, death is called a white event and when a person dies, people come to the funeral ceremony wearing white. *Po* has the spiritual energy of Lung to make the energy of the Lung descend.

The ancient shamans observed the sun descending in the West in the evening time. After the sun descended, it was no longer visible in the sky but they could see the moon. From this, they understood that the moon is the reflection of the sun. To learn about the moon is a way to learn about the sun since the moon represents the descending part of the sun. The spiritual energy of the Lung system is similar to the spiritual energy of the moon. Ancient shamans gave the moon the same spiritual name *Po*, which is the spiritual name for the Lung as well as the spiritual energy of the moon. The Lung system is associated with the western direction and the Metal element. Evening is the Lung system activity time.

When a person's *Po* energy decreases, the lower level will affect the Lung function and the person may suffer from sadness, grief, congestion, or other Lung diseases because the Lung descending function has a problem. Once the *Po* separates from the Lung, the person will experience many difficulties and strong mental problems may develop. People with strong *Po* energy are likely to have strong life energy and self-confidence and will be able to perform very well.

6.7.4 *Yi* 意 — Will

The spiritual energy of the Spleen system is *Yi*. The Chinese character *Yi* is composed of the upper radical *Yin* 音 for voice and the lower radical *Xin* 心 for Heart. The voice is the sound of the Heart. This means the energy of the Will is related to the Heart. *Yi* also means recall and this is the function of the Spleen as well. Spleen belongs to the Earth element and it is the coordinator of the body. The spiritual energy of Spleen *Yi* is connected with the whole body system.

As we discussed in Part II, 6.3 *Wu* 巫 — Chinese Shamanism, the ancient shamans regarded the body as the center of the universe. They also considered the Earth, on which they resided, to be the central planet of the universe. They saw the sun and moon as surrounding the Earth and regarded the Earth as the coordinator. They understood that the spiritual energy of the Earth is similar to the spiritual energy of the Spleen system in the body.

When a person's *Yi* energy decreases, the lower level will affect the Spleen function. The person may have a reduced appetite and low energy, and may also be physically weak or have digestive function problems because the Spleen function is weak. Once the *Yi* separates from the Spleen, the person may experience severe physical problems in the body such as diabetes, cancer, or Alzheimer's disease. People with strong *Yi* energy will feel physically strong and vibrant.

6.7.5 *Zhi* 志 — Memory

The spiritual energy of the Kidney system is *Zhi*. The Chinese character *Zhi* is composed of the upper radical *Shi* 士 for great person and the lower radical *Xin* 心 for Heart. The symbolic meaning of great person is the ancestral energy of the human being. The *Zhi* energy is related to the Heart. The spiritual energy of Kidney *Zhi* is the memory of the ancestral energy of the human being, which records who we are and where we are from. It is the reservoir of life energy. The Kidney belongs to the Water element and is associated with the northern direction.

The ancient shamans observed nature and understood that most of the Earth is water and that Water is the first element of the Earth. They understood that water has the special function of carrying the universal energy and also carries information from the primordial cosmos. They knew that life started in water. Since they lived in the northern hemisphere, they saw that the northern region was covered with ice and understood that the frozen state of water is the prenatal stage of life. That is the reason that the north direction is associated with the Water element. The ancient shamans saw that the spiritual energy of Water is equal to the spiritual energy of the Kidney system in the body. Kidney is the root of the prenatal body.

When a person's *Zhi* energy decreases, the lower level will affect the Kidney function and the person may have lower back pain, leg pain, poor memory, and fear because the Kidney storing or memory function is weak. Once the *Zhi* separates from the Kidney, the person may be at risk of dying. People with strong *Zhi* energy combined with the Kidney system are likely to have a good memory and strong life energy and be able to accomplish many things.

6.7.6 *Shen* 神 — Spirit

The spiritual energy of the Heart system is *Shen* 神, spirit. The Chinese character *Shen* is composed of the left radical *Shi* 示 for display or guiding, and the right radical *Shen* 申 for stretch or lightning. The radical for display and guiding is symbolic of the light shining down from the sun, moon, and stars. It symbolizes a message from Heaven. The right radical is the original character for spirit. As the spiritual energy of the Heart, *Shen* 神 is the emperor of the body.

The function of *Shen* 神 is to regulate the Heart energy to work in the different parts of the body so that everything functions in an orderly way. The Heart belongs to the Fire element and is associated with the southern direction. Ancient shamans understood there would be no life energy on Earth without Fire. The Water would stay in the ice stage and no life would emerge on Earth because Fire melts ice and creates flowing water, and life starts from the flowing water. Therefore, Fire is the symbol for life.

When a person's *Shen* decreases, the lower level will affect the Heart function and the person may develop a lot of problems. The life energy of the whole body may be in a low state. Once the *Shen* separates from the Heart, the person may die. People with strong *Shen* combined with Heart are likely to be very active and passionate.

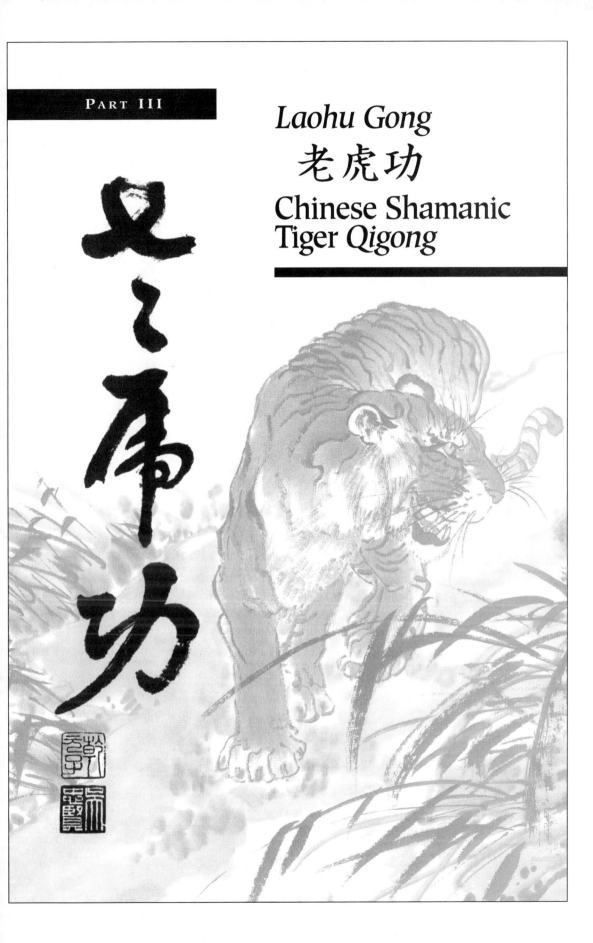

PART III

Laohu Gong

老虎功

Chinese Shamanic
Tiger *Qigong*

The Doorway
of all Mystery[1]

眾妙之門

Zhong Miao Zhi Men

門 **Men**

(Doorway) –
Learn the Name

I n the Chinese tradition, the name of an object symbolizes all the information about that object. For instance, a new baby's name is used not only for communication purposes but also contains the baby's personality and life karma. In Chinese, we have a saying, "A person's name comes from the universe." In other words, it doesn't matter who gave you your name—the universe is the original source of your name. The same is true for the names of *Qigong* forms. The name of the form is the essence and spirit of the form. Gaining a better understanding of the name will help us in our practice.

The original Chinese name for this *Qigong* form is *Laohu Gong* 老虎功, Shamanic Tiger *Qigong*.

7.1 To Be "Old"

Lao 老 literally means old. In Chinese, it is a symbol for wisdom. Of course, we all know that a person doesn't have to be old to be wise. However, even now in modern China, "old" is used as a title to express respect. For instance, the Chinese word for teacher is *Laoshi* 老師– which translates directly into English as "old master." In Chinese tradition, teaching is one of the most respected jobs. The function of a teacher used to be described as "Pass the Dao, teach techniques, and help students find the answers to their questions and doubts." [2] No matter how old you were, you were an "old master" if you were a teacher in China. In ancient times, the shaman held the most respected job and teaching was part of the shaman's job.

The ancient oracle bone Chinese writing style can help us better understand *Lao* 老 (old). The written pattern of the oracle bone character for *Lao* looks like a person holding a staff. In Chinese shamanism, a staff represents the power of the universe. With a staff, a shaman had the power to pass on the universal knowledge to others. Later, when teachers took over part of the shaman's job, they always taught with a small staff in their hands like the shaman. The first time I looked at this oldest style of Chinese character, an image arose in my mind: the Queen Mother of the West (*Xiwangmu* 西王母) standing on the top of Kunlun Mountain with the victory staff in her hand.

Oracle bone style of Chinese character for *Lao* 老 (old).

7.2 Holding *Zheng Qi* 正气

Hu 虎 means tiger. The tiger is a symbol for shamanic power and for *Qi*, especially *Zhengqi* 正气 (righteous or correct *Qi*). *Qi* can be translated as vital energy or vital breath. Usually, the Chinese call the tiger *Laohu* 老虎 —literally meaning "old tiger," regardless of the tiger's age. The tiger is the spiritual animal of the western direction and is related to the Queen Mother of the West (See Part II, 4.2.1 *Xiwangmu* 西王母—Queen Mother of the West). The Queen Mother of the West is a condensation of the Subtlest Vital Breath of the Western Essence from the Vital Breath of the Dao of the Original Chaos. This is the source of the name of this book, ***The Vital Breath of the Dao***.

The tiger is the spiritual animal of the western direction and is related to the Queen Mother of the West.

The universal rhythm of the Dao can be found in the microcosm of the Lung. From a classical Chinese medicine perspective, we will never get sick if we can maintain *Zhengqi* in the body. Physically, *Zhengqi* is represented most strongly by the Lung, which prevents *Xie* 邪 (evil) *Qi* from invading the body. Here, *Zheng* 正 can be translated as correct or upright. In contrast to *Zheng*, *Xie* can be translated as incorrect or tilted. Therefore, *Xieqi* includes all the factors, such as emotions, food, weather, habits, attitude, posture, or trauma, that may cause illness. One of the functions of Lung is to govern and energize all the meridians of the body. Strong Lung *Qi* helps us maintain wellness. We will be more susceptible to illness if the Lung *Qi* is weak. Thus, in Chinese medicine, the tiger is the spiritual animal of Lung and stands for the essential Lung *Qi* and vital breath.

Gong 功 originally meant hard work. In our context, it means a *Qigong* form.

For further details about the tiger, the Queen Mother of the West, *Qi*, and *Gong*, please read Part II *Han San He Yi* 含三合一 — Holding Three in One (The Fundamentals of Chinese Shamanic *Qigong*) of this book.

Laohu Gong 老虎功 translates into English as Chinese Shamanic Tiger *Qigong*. The form is based on symbolic power—the essence of Chinese Shamanism—and has both medical and martial arts applications. The tiger form is the story of energy circulation from West to East, the movement of the Dao itself, as the symbolic power of the tiger communicates directly with the Dao. Through regular practice of the tiger form, one will tonify one's *Zhengqi* and increase the harmonizing *Qi* of the whole body. In this way, one will be able to attune the personal *Qi* to resonate with the Universal *Qi*, to discover one's true potential nature, and to breathe with the Dao.

根 *Gen*

(Root) – The Background

8.1 *Emei Zhengong* 峨嵋真功

Laohu Gong (Chinese Shamanic Tiger *Qigong*) is from the *Emei Zhengong* (Mt. Emei Sage Style *Qigong*) school. Mt. Emei Sage Style *Qigong* combines the traditions of ancient shamanism, Confucianism, Daoism, classical Chinese medicine, and the martial arts. The elements of this style are rooted in the ancient world of Chinese shamanism, which is the source of all the classical Chinese traditions. In ancient China, shamans were respected as sages, and sages were shamans.

The theoretical foundation of the Mt. Emei Sage Style *Qigong* is rooted in *Yijing* science and the principles of classical Chinese medicine. Generally, we can classify this style as a type of Confucian *Qigong* since all of the forms contain the rational and moral meanings of the Confucian perspective. This style can also be categorized as belonging to the *Fulu* 符箓 School because it holds to some rituals and methods that are similar to those in the Daoist *Fulu* tradition. The Chinese character *Fu* 符 means symbol, omen, in alignment with, or in accord with. *Lu* 箓 refers to the book of prophecy, incantation, or a Daoist amulet (a charm to ward off evil). Because of its ancient shamanic ritual practices, the *Fulu* 符籙 School has been described as a shamanic school. We can also consider it to be a classical Chinese medical *Qigong* school due to its inclusion of strong medical functions.

8.2 Union

The most prominent feature of the Mt. Emei Sage Style *Qigong* is union, a concept that dates back to ancient Chinese civilization. In his book, *Peasant Society and Culture*, sociologist Robert Redfield explains that in any civilization, both great and little traditions exist. "The great tradition is cultivated in schools or temples; the little tradition works itself out and keeps itself going in the lives of the unlettered in their village communities."[3] The two traditions are interdependent. The Mt. Emei Sage style of *Qigong*, along with other classical styles of *Qigong*, can be considered a little tradition while Daoism and Confucianism can be considered great traditions. The great and little traditions have long affected each other in China. The great tradition was formed from the little tradition and then became the main momentum in the development of Chinese civilization. Great or little, the core feature of all Chinese traditions is union rather than separation.

Many aspects of Chinese culture (music, art, medicine, science, etc.) are attributed to a single great tradition when, in truth, other traditions contributed to their development as well. For instance, the *Yijing* (I Ching or Book of Changes) is regarded as the most revered classic of Confucianism. It would be incorrect, however, to think that the *Yijing* is based solely on Confucianism since Daoism contains most of the pragmatic methods of *Yijing* science, such as Chinese Five Elements Astrology, *Fengshui*, and various divination methods.

Confucianism and Daoism, the two main pillars of classical Chinese tradition, both originated in the ancient world of shamanism. As the way of humanity, Confucianism inherited and rationalized the knowledge of courtesy, ceremonial rites and regulations, and aspects of personal emotion from the ancient shamanic rituals. As the way of nature, Daoism rationalized and expanded the wisdom of the way of the universe and applied pragmatic knowledge from the ancient shamanic rituals.[4]

Another important classical Chinese tradition is classical Chinese medicine (CCM). It represents the joining of Daoism and Confucianism and is thoroughly based on *Yijing* science. The *Tang* 唐 Dynasty (617–907 CE) sage *Sun Simiao* 孫思邈, who is respected as the "Medical King" by the Chinese, stated that "nobody qualifies to be a master physician without knowledge of the science of change."[5] Indeed, CCM and Chinese shamanism are widely considered to have originated from the same source. In Chinese, the term is 巫醫同源 *Wu Yi Tong Yuan*, which translates literally as "shaman and doctor come from the same source." In fact, many of the ancient documents verify that ancient Chinese doctors were shamans.[6]

From this we can conclude that shamanism, Confucianism, Daoism, and classical Chinese Medicine connect to each other to form a union—and union is the prominent feature of the classical Chinese traditions. Through the *Qigong* form, we will come to see this feature more clearly even though we will not discuss the martial arts application of the Tiger form in this book.

HALF PRICE BOOKS

1375 W. Lane Ave
Columbus, OH 43221
614-486-8765

03/31/09 04:56 PM
#00052/SMOH052/00001

CUSTOMER: 0000000000
SALE: 0001102977

...305 (used books at low prices)

IP/HAND	0.00
X (6.75% on $4.19)	0.28
TAL	4.47

PAYMENT TYPE

SH		5.03

YMENT TOTAL	$	5.03
ANGE DUE - CASH	$	0.56

THANK YOU!

The perfect gift...HPB Gift Cards.
Choose any amount for any occasion.

END OF TRANSACTION

REFUND POLICY

Cash refunds and charge card credits on all merchandise* are available within 7 days of purchase with receipt. Merchandise charged to a credit card will be credited to your account. Exchange or store credit will be issued for merchandise returned within 30 days with receipt. Cash refunds for purchases made by check are available after twelve (12) business days and are then subject to the time limitations stated above. Please include original packaging and price tag when making a return. Proper I.D. and phone number may be required, where permitted. We reserve the right to limit or decline refunds.

*Gift cards cannot be returned for cash, except as required by law.

REFUND POLICY

Cash refunds and charge card credits on all merchandise* are available within 7 days of purchase with receipt. Merchandise charged to a credit card will be credited to your account. Exchange or store credit will be issued for merchandise returned within 30 days with receipt. Cash refunds for purchases made by check are available after twelve (12) business days and are then subject to the time limitations stated above. Please include original packaging and price tag when making a return. Proper I.D. and phone

抖 *Dou*

(Shaking) — The Ritual of Heart

9.1 Inner Dancing and Drumming

In the *Emei Zhengong School*, before practicing *Qigong* forms, we usually start with *Dou* 抖—shaking. Shaking is reminiscent of shamanic dancing and drumming. The ancient shamans regarded the Universal *Qi* (energy) as a harmonious musical rhythm, the universal vibration. Shaking focuses the body and *Shen* 神 (spirit) on the universal vibrations we are experiencing. This is a way to awaken the energy and consciousness in the body. Most people do not realize that there is a subtle energy—*Qi*—accompanying them through their entire lives. Some people will never believe the existence of this kind of energy in the body because they have never experienced it. This shaking movement can help us open our energy gates and meridians—the energy channels in the body. It allows the free flow of *Qi* to connect with universal energy for moving into the basic *Qi* state.

In addition, we can learn to open our hearts to feel the connection between ourselves and nature through further practice. As we learned in Part II, 6.3.3 The Function of *Wu* 巫, dancing and drumming are shamanic methods to understand the *Shen*. Even the shamans of today use the ritual of dancing to facilitate universal connections, such as bringing rain to dry farmland. In Chinese shamanic *Qigong* practice, shaking is the inner dancing and drumming to access our inner great medicine—energetic rhythm for healing and achieving Enlightenment.

Let's take a look at the Chinese character *Yao* 藥 (medicine) to get a feel for this rhythm. The character *Yao* is composed of two parts: a radical meaning grass or herb on top and the character 樂 for music at bottom. In addition to carrying the meaning of medicine or cure, this character can stand for music itself, happiness, or enjoyment. The ancient sages spoke of music as an analogy for universal energy. Harmony is derived from the resonance of sacred sounds. Harmony is also the connection and response of different entities. In other words, the energy created by resonating in harmony with the universe is the original medicine.[7]

Dancing and music are forms of vibration, as is shaking. When practicing *Qigong*, we always begin with shaking in order to open the pores, connect with the *Shen* and *Qi* fields, and communicate with the universe. During the shaking, we also use different sounds or mantras to open the meridians and all the cells of the body to connect with the universal energies and harmonize with the Universal *Qi*. This process in *Qigong* is no different from the *Wu* rituals of dancing and drumming: through vibration and special frequencies, the *Wu* connect with the Universal *Qi*, their own spirits, and high-level beings.

9.2 Awaken Your Consciousness

Step 1

In a standing position, bring your feet together, maintaining contact with the ground. Keep your body erect, arms hanging loosely by your sides with your fingers pointing down. Keep your armpits open, imagining tennis balls in your armpits. Your chin is slightly lowered. Close your eyes, placing the tip of your tongue on the tooth ridge just behind your teeth.

Visualize the upper half of your body reaching into Heaven and the lower half rooting into Earth. See your arms extending deep into the Earth with your fingers reaching to the center of the Earth. Pull the Earthly *Yin Qi* from the center of the Earth and feel it filling your whole body.

See the sun and moon. See the Big Dipper. Go from the Big Dipper to the North Star and feel the connection between the North Star and the *Baihui* (100 meetings) point (GV-20) on the crown of your head. Feel the Universal Qi pouring into your body through the *Baihui* point and filling up your whole body with Heavenly *Qi*. See the planets and feel yourself connecting with each of them. Concentrate on your *Dantian* and see it as a small sun or ball of fire in your lower abdomen.

Step 2

Step to the right, feet shoulder-width apart. Rise up onto the balls of your feet and raise your arms above your shoulders, palms up. Hold your breath for a few seconds, then sink down into a low squat, bringing the arms to shoulder level. Jump into the air while circling the arms up and around and down in front of the *Dantian*. Start shaking your whole body, bouncing about and breathing into the *Dantian* with *Heng* 哼 (Hung) breaths. Take in the lineage and Universal *Qi* via the pores of your whole body. Use *Heng* on the out-breath to concentrate *Qi* in the lower *Dantian*. As you move faster and faster, the ball/sun of your *Dantian* becomes denser and denser.

As you continue shaking, think of your body parts:

First think about the Heavenly Gate (*Baihui*). Open this gate further to receive Heavenly *Qi*.

Then think about each of your eyes, your nose, mouth, face, neck, shoulders, heart, lungs, spine, hips, spleen, stomach, pancreas, bladder, liver, gall bladder, intestines, legs, ankles, and feet.

Then, shake the whole body in a freestyle manner.

Gradually slow down and then stop. Bring your hands up over the crown of your head and down in front of the body on both sides. Relax. Feel the tingling.

Feel the warmth, or even heat, in your body. Feel the light entering and nourishing your whole body as if you are taking a *Qi* shower. Then move your consciousness to your lower *Dantian*—concentrate the energy there. Observe the inner landscape of your body with your inner eye. At this moment, you may have special experiences in your body and spirit.

10

澂
Fa

(The Way) – Shamanic Tiger *Qigong* Movements

10.1 *Hong Meng Yi Qi* 鴻蒙一炁
—Return to the Great Primordial *Qi*

Meaning: *Hong* means great, big, or vast. *Meng* means unknown, vague, or moistening. *Meng* is also the name of Hexagram Four, Mountain over Water in the *Yijing*. This hexagram is a picture of a fresh spring at the foot of the mountain. This is a good *Qi* field in which to live and grow. The function of *Meng* is to nourish and create *Zhengqi* (righteous *Qi*). "The Superior Person refines his character by being thorough in every activity," according to the *Yijing*. *Meng* can also mean unclear, enshrouded in fog, and moisture. *Yi* means One, the state of oneness of the universe. *Qi* is the vital energy or breath. In terms of Chinese cosmology, the primordial universe was one big ball of *Qi* in the beginning. The Tiger form is patterned after the movement of *Qi*. According to *Yijing* principles,

Heaven is classified as Metal *Qi*, and through making the first movement in the Tiger form, we connect with the Metal *Qi*, the primordial life energy. In other words, we move into a primordial universe state where all is one. **Hong Meng Yi Qi**, then, means return to the primordial or original universe state.

Movement: Stand with your feet together and your toes grabbing the Earth. Straighten your back so it is solid like a mountain. Lift your perineum to seal the *Dihu* 地户 (Earthly Door, CV1). Pull the lower abdomen in. Open your chest.

Straighten your neck and keep your head upright. Imagine your head touching Heaven with the *Tianmen* 天門 (Heavenly Gate, GV20) open. Put the tip of your tongue on the tooth ridge behind your teeth. Close your teeth and mouth. Keep your shoulders down, your arms relaxed, and your armpits open. Open your hands with fingers straight. Close your eyes with eyelids relaxed. Take your eyesight within. Listen within to sense the *Qi* state.

Visualization: With your eyes closed, look and listen within to sense the *Qi* state. Feel your body split from your waist, with your upper body suspended through the *Tianmen* and your lower body rooted into the Earth. Feel the Heavenly and Earthly energies penetrate to mix in the *Dantian*. Imagine the Universal *Qi* as light surrounding your body. Open all the pores of the body, allowing the Universal *Qi* to pour into your body. Feel your body merging with the *Qi* and returning to the state of primordial universe *Qi*.

Breathing: Breathe through your nose. Adjust your breathing to be slow, smooth, deep, and even. There should be no noise from your breathing. In Chinese, this breathing technique is called *Mi Mi Mian Mian* 密密綿綿, meaning the breath is soft and unbroken like cotton and silk. Gather the *Qi* with all the pores of your body as you inhale. Condense the *Qi* in your *Dantian* 丹田 as you exhale.

Function: This movement appears to do nothing, but it is doing a great deal because it is a way to help you awaken your original life source, and it is creating and nourishing the *Zhengqi* (life force). This movement opens the body and enables us to connect with the Universal *Qi*. It also helps us learn about the union of the physical body and the spiritual body. Daily practice of the movement strengthens our vital energy and is good for rebuilding our life energy from a state of weakness.

10.2 *Shui Hu Jue Xing* 睡虎覺醒
—Sleeping Tiger Wakes Up

Meaning: *Shui* means sleep or unknown. *Hu* means tiger. In Chinese, another name for tiger is *Dachong* 大虫 . *Dachong* literally means big or great worm. There is a symbolic connection between the tiger and the worm. The symbolic meaning of worm in Chinese shamanism is strong life energy, no stagnation. This strong life energy is apparent when we cut a worm in half. It can still move and it can regenerate itself into two worms. *Jue* means wisdom or Enlightenment. *Xing* means to wake up. *Shui Hu* means sleeping tiger and is a symbol for an unenlightened person. Everyone has the capacity to be enlightened. However, we may never discover this quality and cultivate it if our consciousness is buried in a busy, customary, routine-filled life. This movement, which imitates a tiger waking up, represents awakening our deep consciousness and potential energy in the body. Through practice and discipline—daily cultivation—we work with the three treasures, the best medicine in the body: *Jing* (essence), *Qi* (vital energy), and *Shen* (spirit). This movement teaches us that the original function of *Qigong* practice is a way of achieving Enlightenment.

Movement: Feel the weight and power of the tiger's bones and muscles—your bones and muscles. Your fingers should be curled like tiger claws as your hands move. This is important for holding the energy. (The acupuncture points on the extremities are located on the border where microcosmic energy meets macrocosmic energy.) Move your whole body, including your legs, and feel yourself undulate with the martial power of the tiger. When you feel you have become the tiger, undulate the whole body from the *Dantian* with toes grabbing the floor. Move your arms like waves, with your fingers curled into tiger claws. The tiger looks heavy but moves fast. The tiger is very sensitive and agile.

Visualization: Imagine you are a tiger waking up from a deep sleep. Begin connecting with the energy of the tiger. Become the tiger. Feel the joints of the body opening. Feel the whole body moving freely without stagnation, moving like a worm.

Breathing: Regulate your breath as you did in the first movement and start moving your body. Then you can modify your breathing to imitate a tiger yawning. Take a deep breath and make soft growling noises like a tiger.

Function: This movement releases *Qi* stagnation and strengthens the Liver function thereby improving the flexibility of the whole body. It helps us to awaken and to understand the energy in our deeper layers—that energy which is usually never accessed or used by the conscious mind. By doing this form, we will become deeply aware of the presence of the special treasures of the body: *Jing, Qi,* and *Shen.*

10.3 *Li Di Bai Wei* 立地摆尾
—Tiger Wags its Tail

Meaning: *Li* means standing or establish. *Di* means Earth. *Li Di* means standing on the Earth or building up Earth energy in the body. It is a symbol of being rooted. Our practice or cultivation needs to be grounded. The state of being grounded is the symbolic meaning of the tiger as well. The tiger is a symbol of status and also carries the meaning of knowing one's rank, place, and position. Although the tiger is powerful when moving, he is most often found "sitting in place," "dwelling at home," or "presiding from his lair" while surveying his kingdom, acutely aware of everything going on below. Learning "who I am" and "where I belong" (i.e., location and position) will help us ground. We need to be in the moment and we need to connect with life around us. The pattern of the tiger skin itself also represents the Dao. In other words, the Dao is very close—life and spiritual cultivation should not be separated. *Bai Wei* means wagging the tail. The tail represents the power of the tiger—it is from here that the tiger derives its power. *Bai Wei* is a symbol for pride. The acts of practice and cultivation are venerable and we should be proud of them.

Movement: As you breathe in, step to the right and make a wide horse stance. Bring your left hand up in front of your mouth as your right hand swings behind you. Straighten your arms and pay attention to the palms. Be sure they are in the center line of your body. Focus on your tailbone. The tailbone, which is the end of the spine, is the secret source of life power. Breathe out and shake your tailbone. Repeat this sequence of shaking on this side five times. Five is an Earth number and represents the Five Elements. After repeating the sequence five times, switch arms and do the same movement on the other side. Do three rounds of this movement. Three is the number of creation, symbolizing the three layers: Heaven, Earth, and the Human Being. Together, these three layers represent the universe.

Visualization: Imagine you are a tiger standing with feet rooting into the Earth. Wag the tail, focusing on the tailbone as you wag your hips. Feel the momentum from your tiger tailbone.

Breathing: Take a deep, sharp breath before shaking the tailbone. Then breathe out with the sound *Heng* 哼 (Hung) as you are shaking.

Function: This movement enhances the *Zhongqi* 中氣, the central energy of the body, and includes the Earth element and its harmonizing function. It is good for healing any digestive or Earth pathology. Since Earth (*Tu* 土) is the mother of Metal (*Jin* 金), it is logical to begin with the root of Metal in this form. This movement is a way to build up the Earth energy (physical health, mental stability, and harmonizing function) before we play with the Metal animal, tiger.

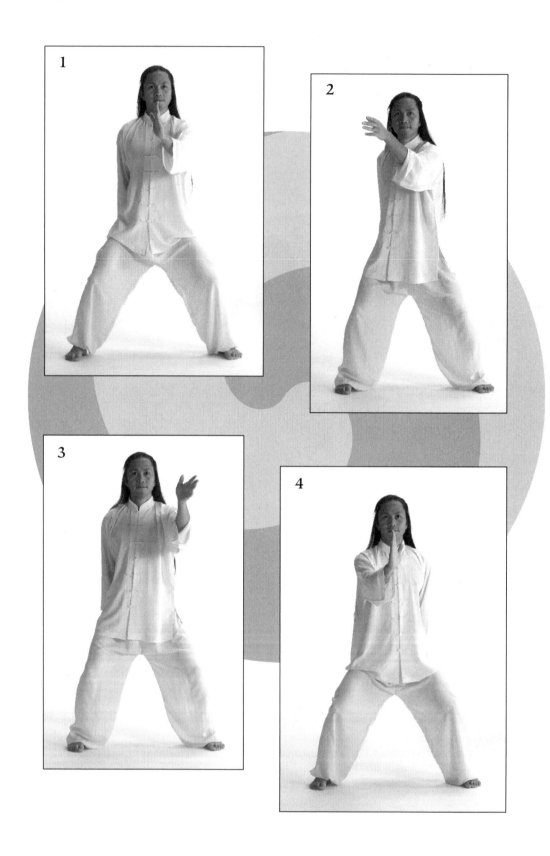

10.4 *Dan Dan Chu Dong* 眈眈出洞 —Tiger Emerges from the Cave

Meaning: *Dan Dan* means glare, gaze, or stare. Eyes represent the spiritual window of the soul. When we start our practice, we are opening our spiritual windows to connect with the outer world and to learn the way of the universe. This movement is the pattern of the tiger's eyes—open and staring fiercely. *Chu* means come out or emerge. *Dong* means cave—the tiger's home and also the first humans' home. The tiger is the epitome of the wild animal, displaying powerful survival instincts and a need for freedom. The tiger needs "breathing space" and the freedom to roam and defend vast territories. This movement is a symbol for open space or an open heart. In *Qigong* practice, we should learn how to open the spiritual window of the Heart-Mind, not merely remain in a small cave.

Movement: Ending with your right hand out in front of you after the third round of "Tiger Wags its Tail," allow your right arm and hand, with palm down, to come to a 90-degree angle. Simultaneously, bring your left arm around from behind, rotating your left palm down. Turn your right arm, bringing the palm up, and allow the right arm to pass over your left arm, eventually ending with your left hand, palm down, under your right elbow. All of this is done as you are pivoting to the left. The arms cooperate with each other, creating a *Yin-Yang* movement. Explore your territory, working the meridians in your arms and feeling the energy. The energy from your right hand and fingers should be penetrating and shooting outward.

Visualization: Extend your fingers far away and feel your fingers touch the ends of the universe. Feel the *Laogong* 勞宮 of your upper hand connect with Heaven as you feel the *Laogong* of your lower hand connect with Earth. Be aware of your eyes perceiving the outside world, seeing far away and taking in everything in the universe.

Breathing: Regulate your breath from the lower *Dantian*. Inhale and exhale, feeling the *Qi* rotate in your lower *Dantian*. Visualize the breath in your lower *Dantian* as a moving *Qi* ball, picturing the *Taiji* symbol for energy circulation.

Function: This movement helps open the four spiritual gates in the body: the two hips and the two shoulders. By circulating the energy in the lower *Dantian*, the energy of the body unites with universal energy. This results in unification rather than separation. The movement is good for strengthening the Heart function or healing any diseases of the limbs.

10.5 *Yao Wu Yang Wei* 耀武揚威 —Tiger Displays Martial Power

Meaning: *Yao* means shining, lightning, show, or display. *Wu* means martial power. Thus, *Yao Wu* means to display one's martial power. *Yang* means show or wave. *Wei* means respect, venerable, or spiritual power. It is a sincere feeling of respect for nature and for our practice. In the traditional way, doing *Qigong* practice is like performing a special ceremony or ritual to connect ourselves with the universe. The tiger displaying its martial power represents bringing out our inner potential for spiritual power. This is a type of spiritual energy that we use for cultivation. In our *Qigong* practice, new challenges are met often, and we need this inner power to display confidence and fortitude.

Movement: Pivot in a slow, relaxed fashion back to the right, suddenly snapping your right wrist so that your right palm is more upward and slightly higher than eye level. Allow your left hand to move down to the lower *Dantian* and connect with Earthly *Qi*. Work the meridians in your arms and legs, twisting and undulating, feeling the power and strength of the tiger. Feel your *Qi* move through all parts of your tiger body, even to the tips of each body hair.

Visualization: Imagine being a dragon. Feel your whole body moving—not just the wrists and hands. Your whole body spirals, and the *Qi* condenses into the bone and marrow (*Qi Lian Ru Gu* 气斂入骨). At the same time, feel as if each hair on the body is like a needle or an iron weapon standing straight up.

Breathing: Allow your breath to be slow, smooth, deep, and even. Breathe with all the pores of the body, not with just the lungs. Occasionally, you can make a slow inhale followed by a sharp exhale with the sound *Heng* 哼 .

Function: This movement connects us with the harmony of the Universal *Qi* and is excellent for dispersing *Qi* stagnation in the body. It also helps strengthen the Kidney and Liver *Qi* and harmonizes the Lung and Liver *Qi*.

10.6 *Shen Jian Zhan Xie* 神劍斬邪
—Spiritual Sword Kills the Demon

Meaning: *Shen* means spirit, divine, or essence. *Jian* is a sword, which is a symbol for wisdom. *Zhan* means cut off with a sharp motion or chop. *Xie* means evil (as in *Xie Qi*), devil, demon, or ghost. *Xie* means all the factors that cause illness. It may be a blockage in your body, problems in your life, unbalanced emotions, or anything that pulls you away from or blocks you from your endeavors. In our *Qigong* practice, we always feel resistance—this is the evil *Qi* that makes us feel that it is all right not to practice. If we don't have wisdom, we follow this "outside face" that is beautiful and alluring but keeps us from moving forward. The spiritual sword represents special wisdom which we need for cutting off the evil energy. Through practice, we will become stronger physically and spiritually. We must develop the ability to kill the inner demons that prevent us from moving into a better state. The symbolic meaning of this movement is that new spiritual life will be born through the kill.

Movement: Keeping your left foot immobile, slowly pivot on the ball of your right foot as your right hand floats up above your head, stirring the Heavens. Your left hand remains at the level of your *Dantian*. Once your body has turned to the left, reposition your left foot so that your toes are facing left. Then, slice your right hand downward suddenly like a cosmic sword full of *Qi* to below your waist as your left hand comes up to your chin with the palm out to guard.

Visualization: Imagine that your hands and arms are swords made of sharp, hard, righteous metal. When the hands cross, they move in a scissoring action, as if two swords are cooperating to release everything created from the old evil energy. Envision driving off the evil energy. The "fight" here is not with another entity, but with our deeper heart ego. The practice helps us to realize the "evil" part hidden inside our own hearts that we must drive away. It is important to understand that this tendency exists in all of us. Merely following our feelings does not always lead us down the right path.

Breathing: Inhale as your arms open. As your arms cross, exhale. At the end of the exhale, make a *Heng* sound with your mouth closed. You can do two or three *Heng* sounds in quick succession.

Function: This movement benefits the shoulders. It can help release a frozen shoulder or other shoulder conditions. It is a way to strengthen your healing power and your ability to transmit external *Qi*. You can use this movement to drive off disease. The *Heng* sound has the function of releasing evil *Qi*, with or without the body movement. It is especially good for Heart and *Shen*.

10.7 *Qi Hua San Pan* 气化三盘
—*Qi* Transforms the Three Layers

Meaning: *Qi* is the vital energy of nature. **Hua** means change or transformation. It is a process that changes matter from one state to another. It is like a worm (caterpillar) transforming into a butterfly. We call this process **Hua**. **Qi Hua** in *Qigong* practice means that *Qi* may be used to remove blockages to allow the energy to flow. This is the *Qi* healing skill. After doing *Qigong* practice for a certain length of time, you may use your *Qi* to transform yourself or to transform another person's disease to flowing *Qi*. **San** means three. **Pan** means plate, layer, or circle. It also means something that is coiled together. **San Pan** means the three layers. The three layers have much symbolic meaning. In the body, they relate to the three parts of the body (upper, middle, lower). In terms of energy, they refer to the *Jing*, *Qi*, and *Shen*. In terms of the universe, they refer to Heaven, Earth, and Humanity. All three layers connect with the *Qi* flow. Thus, the symbolism here refers to *Qi* flowing smoothly in the three layers in such a way that there is peace and harmony.

Movement: Rotate back to center, bringing your right arm up as you turn the palm down and turn your left palm up until they meet at head level with your left hand resting under your right elbow. Feel yourself holding a *Qi* ball with your palms. Rotate left and right with your arms, turning your palms over with each shift in direction. Rotate the upper body once at the upper *Dantian*, once at the middle *Dantian* and once at the lower *Dantian*. This represents the harmonizing of Heaven, Earth, and the Human Being.

Visualization: Visualize holding the *Qi* ball with both hands. Imagine extending your fingers to touch the ends of the universe. As your hands move, visualize the *Qi* following the hands and passing through the three layers of Heaven, Earth, and Humanity. Envision cooperation between all three *Dantian*.

Breathing: Inhale deeply before shifting right. Exhale as you shift right and inhale as you shift left.

Function: This movement transforms physical blockages and stagnation, which allows the *Qi* to flow smoothly. It balances the three burners which are equivalent to the three layers: Heaven, Earth, and the Human Being. Diseases that are related to the three burners include heart and lung diseases, gastrointestinal diseases, and kidney diseases. Diseases located in these organs, or burners, may manifest in insomnia, anxiety, chest pain, nausea, and lower back pain. This movement also strengthens the ability to transmit external *Qi* for healing.

10.8 *Tong Tian Che Di* 通天徹地
—Connect with Heaven and Penetrate Earth

Meaning: *Tong* means connect, communicate, pathway, flowing, or circulation. *Tian* means Heaven. *Che* means penetrate, complete, or perfect. *Di* means Earth. *Tong Tian Che Di* is the ability to connect with the universe. The ancient Chinese shamans had the ability to connect with the universe. The human body has the potential to connect with universal energy—this is the dream of freedom in *Qigong* practice. We can harmonize our energy with nature through our cultivation.

Movement: After finishing the third round of harmonizing the three layers, shift your body back to the center. Quickly snap your right wrist out and upward with palm up to Heaven (above *Baihui*, GV 20) as you snap your left hand with palm down and at the level of your lower *Dantian*. Move your hands in a slight rotational movement so that you feel the connection between Heaven and Earth.

Visualization: Visualize your fingertips and the *Laogong* of your right hand connecting with Heaven. The fingertips of your left hand root into and connect with the deepest layers of the Earth. Extend yourself both physically and spiritually. Feel the whole body expanding like a dragon to connect with Heaven and Earth.

Breathing: Allow your breath to be slow, smooth, deep, and even.

Function: This movement can help strengthen our ability to connect with the universal energy. It is a good way to open the different layers of the body. This movement will also enhance the sensation of your fingers and your *Laogong* to receive and transmit external *Qi*. It is beneficial for the Triple Burner and digestion.

10.9 *Huai Bao Ri Yue* 懷抱日月
—Embrace the Sun and Moon

Meaning: *Huai* means chest, hold, or heart. *Bao* means embrace or hug. *Ri* 日 is the sun. *Yue* 月 is the moon. The Chinese character formed by combining the characters for sun and moon is *Ming* 明, which means brightness, light, or Enlightenment. The symbol of the left radical sun is *Yang* and the right radical moon is *Yin*. Sun and moon together mean brightness—the brightness of the Heart to be enlightened. The idea is that the heart of an enlightened being is big enough to hold the sun and moon. The heart also holds the spirit or *Shenming* 神明 —the spiritual light. This movement symbolizes the heart as the residence or palace of the Dao in the body.

Movement: Deepen your horse stance. Turn your arms, bringing your right palm face up at the level of the lower *Dantian* and raising your left hand to the level of the middle *Dantian* with palm facing down. Keeping your *Laogong* connected, open your arms wide with your hands rotating the *Qi* ball between them. Then close your arms and bring your hands back to the previous position. Repeat this movement three times. As you open and close your arms, feel your entire body (especially the *Dantian*) open and close three times to symbolize the three layers of the universe and the three *Dantian*. When performing this movement, make sure that your *Laogong* stay connected at all times to hold the energy.

Visualization: Imagine you are embracing the sun and moon as you open and close your hands. Your left hand is the sun and your right hand is the moon. This is *Yin* and *Yang* combining.

Breathing: Inhale as you open and exhale as you close, creating a big circle with your arms.

Function: This movement strengthens the Heart and Lung functions and strengthens the *Qi*. It opens and sensitizes the *Laogong* to both transmitting and receiving energy. It enables us to better understand the *Yin-Yang* principle.

10.10 *Bao Yi Shang Shan* 抱一上山 —Tiger Climbs the Mountain

Meaning: *Bao* means hold. *Yi* means oneness and it stands for the Dao. Holding the oneness means living in the Dao. *Shang* means elevate, climb, or rise. *Shan* means mountain. The mountain symbolizes *Qi*. Mountains are high and close to Heaven. They are sacred places where hermits engage in spiritual cultivation and connect and communicate with Heaven. The symbolic meaning of this movement is that we should learn how to retreat from a busy life.

Movement: Pivot back to the right with your left palm (*Laogong* 勞宮 – PC 8) connected to the inside of your right elbow (*Shaohai* 少海 – HT 3). Snap your hands forward and form tiger claws with your fingers. The right hand is at about chest level and the left hand is at the level of the lower *Dantian*. Move your hands up and down with the whole body moving in a climbing motion. Again, the energy must be held with the fingers as though they are claws. Pump the *Qi* in your arm and leg meridians.

Visualization: Visualize yourself as a tiger climbing up the mountain. Feel your whole body moving and all the parts cooperating with each other, especially the four limbs and claws. The tiger body is heavy, yet swift, sinuous, and agile. This illustrates *Yin* and *Yang*—lightness and heaviness contained in one being. The heaviness is in the bones—condensed and never yielding. The lightness is in the agility of the movement. The tiger is stable and rooted while at the same time agile and active.

Breathing: Inhale deeply, gathering *Qi* into your lower *Dantian*. Breathe out and make the sound of the tiger growling and roaring.

Function: This movement strengthens the life force, the tendons, and the self-healing power, all of which are related to the East. Physically, it opens all the meridians and joints to allow for the free flow of *Qi*. It is especially good for joint problems and kidney disease.

10.11 *Yu Feng Xia Shan* 御風下山 —Ride the Wind Down the Mountain

Meaning: *Yu* means ride or control. *Feng* means wind. The wind, or air, stands for the *Qi*. The wind follows the tiger. Where there is wind, there is tiger energy. Wind is a reference to the breath of nature, as well as to the naturalness and unrestrained manner of the tiger.[7] Like the wind, the tiger comes and goes as it pleases, showing up suddenly and unexpectedly—sometimes with devastating force. As a pathological influence, wind is "the principal of all diseases," according to the *Huangdi Neijing*, just as the tiger is often regarded as the principal of all vicious and harm-bringing animals. *Xia* means descend, lower, or down. *Shan* means mountain. *Xia Shan* symbolizes the return of the enlightened hermit to civilization. *Yu Feng* literally means riding the wind; in other words, how to control the energy and live in a harmonious state. *Yu Feng* also symbolizes flying.

Ancient shamanic stories tell us that the tiger is a bridge for the human being to reach Heaven. The symbolic meaning of this movement is that a hermit, having attained Enlightenment, descends back down to the mundane world to assist the rest of humanity. After a long stay on the mountain, the hermit has achieved the capability to "fly," but it is time for this enlightened being to remember his or her humanity and help others. In our own cultivation, we need to remember this aspect of being human. In the energetic layers of the body, when you build up stronger *Qi* through your practice, *Qi* will "come down" to help weak parts of the body. This movement is connected with Hexagram 11—*Tai* 泰 , the way of balance and stability.

Movement: Pivot on your right foot to the left, keeping your left foot immobile. Your left hand stays below at the level of the *Dantian* while your right hand floats up to gently stir Heaven and gather the Heavenly *Qi*. Pivot your left heel slightly to the left to allow the right knee room enough to end up in the space just to the left of it. Curl your right wrist downward so that your fingers are pointing into the right shoulder (*Jianjing* 肩井 —GB 21) with the back of your hand pointing toward your right ear. In one swift motion, jab your right hand down in front of your right shoulder towards your left foot (*Yongquan* 湧泉 —KD 1), bring your left hand up to in front of your right cheek and drop

into a deep crouching position with your right knee just to the left of your left heel. Both palms should be facing to the right, claws extended to ward off enemies. As your balance in this position improves, pump up and down with your legs to work the meridians.

Visualization: When starting to transition from climbing the mountain, you stir the wind with your hands. During this movement, feel as if you are riding on the wind and gathering the wind. Visualize feeling very light, as if the body has merged with the *Qi*. Also remember to feel stable and grounded like a tiger. Hold the *Qi*, the wind, for a moment and then descend suddenly and smoothly—there is no blockage between the upper and the lower.

Breathing: Inhale, then exhale with a *Heng* sound when descending.

Function: This movement will help to strengthen the Kidney energy. It is one of the best attack-and-defense positions from a martial arts perspective. It is a way to release stagnation in the physical or spiritual body. Wind can transform. This movement benefits the twelve joints: shoulders, elbows, wrists, hips, knees, and ankles. It is a good way to open your spiritual gates and let the energy flow.

10.12 *Qi Guan Chang Hong* 气贯長虹
—*Qi* Transforms into a Rainbow

Meaning: *Qi* has the same meaning as *Qi* in *Qigong* (vital energy). *Guan* means link or penetrate. *Chang* means long or everlasting. *Hong* means rainbow. In Chinese shamanism, rainbow is a symbol for dragon and it is also a bridge linking Heaven and Earth. This symbolizes strong *Qi* that is capable of creating a union between the human being and nature. The symbolic meaning of this movement is the tiger transforming into the dragon—a change in the pattern. It is the communication between East and West, the harmony of *Yin* and *Yang*.

Movement: Prepare to rise, allow your left hand, which is up by your right cheek, to descend with palm forward. Draw a big arc with your hands and arms, at the same time twisting your body at the waist to come back to center. Palms are forward and up, eventually turning palms up with fingers pointing towards each other. This movement involves only the left wrist turning.

Visualization: As you raise your hands, imagine them full of *Qi* as the rainbow rises from Earth to Heaven.

Breathing: Take a deep breath at the start and exhale as you raise your hands and body.

Function: This movement stretches and opens the meridians and lets the *Qi* flow. It also stretches the tendons and benefits the Liver function.

10.13 *Yun Xing Yu Shi* 雲行雨施
—Moving Clouds Make Rain

Meaning: *Yun* means clouds. *Xing* means move, do, element, or achieve. *Yu* means rain. *Shi* means give or execute. The Chinese concept of clouds and rain contains sexual connotations: clouds and rain are a Chinese traditional synonym for intercourse and represent the way of giving birth to new life. In traditional Chinese literature, intercourse is likened to clouds—clouds are the *Qi* that is produced when Heaven and Earth embrace while ejaculation is equivalent to the bursting of the clouds, bringing forth fertilizing rain. Tigers are indeed known to vocalize most vigorously when mating or fighting over a mate. As *Yang* creatures, tigers exhibit sexual prowess and their body parts are treasured aphrodisiacs. Tigers have frequent intercourse, climaxing in a dramatic ejaculation when the male tiger roars and bites his partner's neck.

This movement is the intercourse of *Yin* and *Yang*—a pattern of harmony. The combination of *Yin* and *Yang* is an expression of the Dao. *Qigong* practice is about harmonizing the *Yin* and *Yang*, which will help maintain our health and vital energy. With the appropriate amount of rain, the Earth will give birth to all things. The pattern of this form is like the clouds making rain.

Movement: Allow your arms to descend with fingers pointed up, relaxing the fingers so they become horizontal at about shoulder level. As you lower your arms to the level of your lower *Dantian*, lower your body to come back into horse stance. You are bringing the Heavenly energy to Earth and connecting Heaven and Earth. It is important not to loosen your arms as they move down; you must hold the energy. Keep your head upright and your upper body straight during the movement.

Visualization: Imagine clouds in the sky above. The clouds become rain that falls down to Earth and invigorates the body.

Breathing: Breathe in while your hands hold at the top for a moment; then exhale and relax as your hands move down.

Function: This is a soft *Yin* movement that nourishes the body. *Yin* nourishes *Yang*. This movement is good for *Yin* deficiency, especially Kidney *Yin* deficiency. It is a way to strengthen your sexual power. It is also good for excess *Yang* conditions, such as insomnia and hypertension. Blood pressure can be reduced even if one simply visualizes rain falling rather than actually doing the movement. This should be done every day to achieve long-term stabilization of blood pressure.

10.14 *Er Long Xi Zhu* 二龍戲珠
—Double Dragons Play with the Pearl

Meaning: *Er* means two or double. *Long* means dragon. *Xi* means to play or perform. *Zhu* means pearl or treasure.

From a Chinese shamanic perspective, the pearl represents storage of all the dragon's power and magic. If the dragon loses its pearl, it will lose all its power and will be unable to make rain or transform. The pearl also represents the finest energy or elixir in internal alchemy, which originated from ancient Chinese shamanism. Refining the pearl or the elixir of our body via *Qigong* cultivation is augmenting the life force—*Jing*, *Qi*, and *Shen*.

The dragon holds the pearl under its chin. In *Qigong* practice, the tongue should always be holding the upper palate; it is symbolic of holding the pearl. This is one of the important techniques for making the elixir (in internal alchemy), the internal harmonizing of *Yin* and *Yang*. This whole movement plays with the *Qi*.

Movement: Rotate your wrists and turn your palms up. Extend your arms behind you. Rotate your wrists again to come forward with your *Laogong* facing Heaven. This is a spiral motion and you will raise your hands above your head, fingers pointing to each other, palm up. Both arms are like double dragons spiraling and raising the pearl toward Heaven. Remember, palms should always be facing up during this movement as you repeat it again and again

Visualization: Visualize your hands holding the Pearl / *Qi* ball to refine your external *Qi* and healing capability. Visualize the two arms as two flying dragons playing with the Pearl / *Qi* ball.

Breathing: Start taking a deep breath when your arms are at the lowest point, then continue inhaling and raise your arms up toward Heaven. Keep inhaling until the arms reach as far as they can over the head. Exhale on the way down.

Function: This movement helps open the meridians and refines the *Qi*. It is a great way to strengthen your external *Qi* and healing power. It is especially good for your shoulders, arms, and Triple Burner. It also opens the spine and benefits all the problems related with the spine.

10.15 *Ti Hu Guan Ding* 醍醐灌頂 —Heavenly Dew Purifies the Body

Meaning: *Ti Hu* refers to refined milk, a substance that is powerfully nutritious. For the purpose of our practice, the nutrition referred to here is spiritual nourishment. *Guan* means to pour. *Ding* refers to the top of your head. This movement is a way to open the gate of wisdom, symbolizing not only the way of physical wellness resulting from *Qigong* but also the way of spiritual Enlightenment. It also means the pleasure of receiving wisdom, like pouring rich liqueur over your head.

Movement: Rotate your hands toward Heaven to gather the Universal *Qi* and then turn the palms down so they are facing your head. You can hold this posture for a few minutes. Lower your hands—descending, purifying, and rooting into the Earth with the *Qi*. End with your hands at the level of the lower *Dantian*.

Visualization: Imagine bringing the dew from Heaven into your body and down to Earth. This Heavenly dew is pouring through the top of your head to nourish the body and spirit. It is an inner shower of purification.

Breathing: Inhale and rotate your hands over your head, then exhale as you turn your palms down to face the Earth. Hold your posture and regulate your breathing to be slow, smooth, deep, and even. Make the *Heng* sound as you bring your hands down.

Function: This movement purifies the physical body as well as the energetic Heart. Its function is to move one into a deeper layer of meditation. Your consciousness will be in a high energetic state. One phenomenon of this state in your body is that your saliva (Heavenly dew) will be more refined, more abundant, and will produce a special calming smell. It will purify and nourish the body and *Shen*.

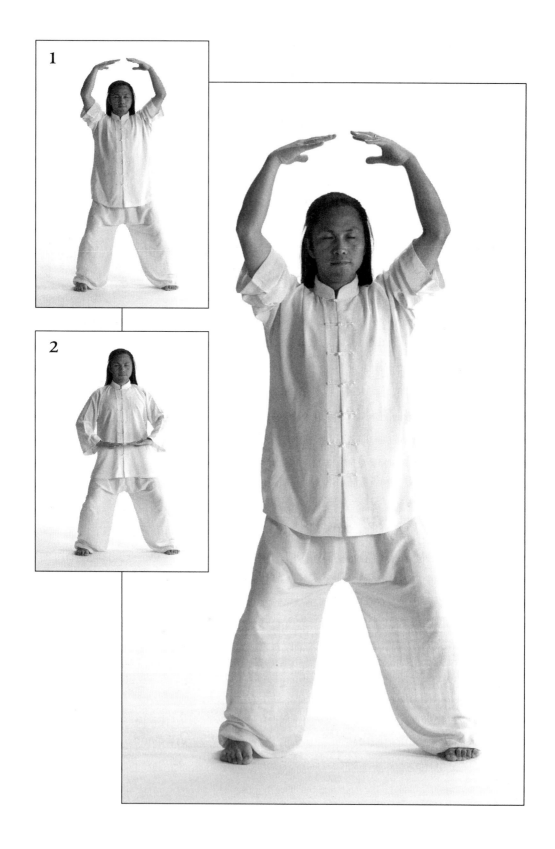

10.16 *Jin Gui Xia Hai* 金龜下海
—Golden Turtle Plunges into the Ocean

Meaning: *Jin* means metal, gold, or golden color. *Gui* means turtle. Turtles can find their way back to the place where they were born no matter how far away it is. Turtles also have the innate ability to navigate long routes in the ocean, and they always remember the origin of their journeys. Turtles are water animals but their shells are like armor, which symbolizes protective energy (*Wei Qi*) and thereby relates the turtle to the Metal element (Metal generates Water). Turtles have the ability to go for indeterminate amounts of time without food, taking *Qi* from the air. The Golden Turtle is a symbol for longevity, the northern direction, and the spiritual energy related to the prenatal energy of the Kidney. *Xia* means plunge into, submerge, lower, reduce, or descend. *Hai* means sea or ocean. Water is the prenatal root of life on Earth and memory. This movement is a symbol for returning to the Dao, and it is related to the shamanic way of understanding the cycles of life and death. It imitates a turtle and it is good for helping us remember who we are since it is a way to discover our universal lineage and roots.

Movement: Take a deep breath and allow yourself to open, feeling your fingers touch the ends of the universe as you gather the Universal *Qi*. Your toes are still grabbing the ground, your back is bent slightly forward from the waist, and all the muscles in your hips are tight. This position mimics the turtle swimming in the ocean. Rotate your fingers toward the *Mingmen* and gather the *Qi* in your kidneys with the mantra of *Hai* or *Hei*. Your *Laogong* are pointing at each kidney as you make the mantra.

Visualization: Imagine yourself as a turtle plunging into the ocean, navigating underwater to find your way home. Gather the *Qi* and essence of the ocean as your *Laogong* point to your kidney, storing the *Qi* and *Jing* (essence) there.

Breathing: Take a deep breath and inhale as you open your arms. Exhale as your fingers reach behind you. Make the *Hai* or *Hei* mantra with your fingers pointing to your kidneys.

Function: This movement works with *Shen* energy to tonify (strengthen) the Heart. It works to tonify the Kidney and to dispel all diseases related to Kidney, such as lower back pain, knee pain, and leg pain. It is good for people who have poor memories. It teaches us about two treasures: *Jing* (essence) of the prenatal body and Water in our daily lives. These are the roots of our spiritual cultivation. (See Part II, 6.7.5 *Zhi* 志 — Memory)

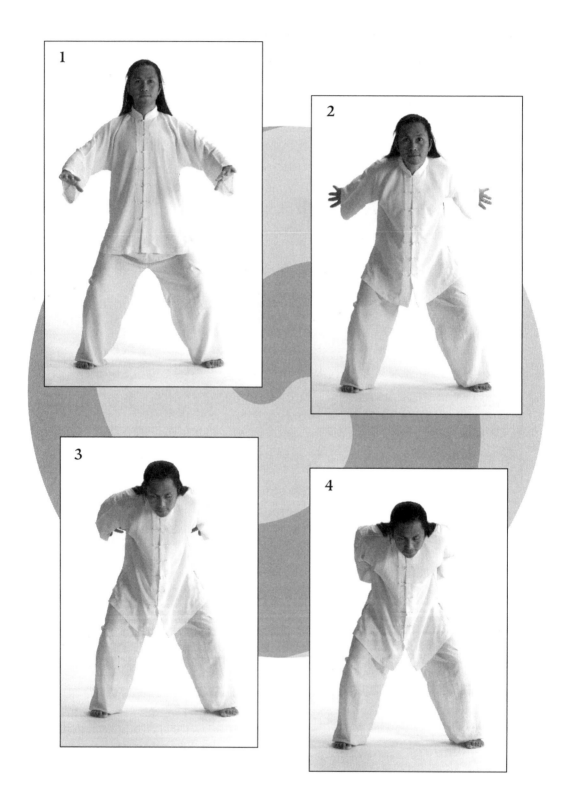

10.17 *Jin Tao Hui Dang* 錦濤回蕩 —Colorful Wave Cleanses the Spirit

Meaning: *Jin* means colorful or brocade. *Tao* means wave or tide. *Hui* means return. *Dang* means wash away or rush. This movement symbolizes purification, as in the ocean's ability to purify the land. Here, we are returning to purify deeper layers of the body—the emotional and spiritual layers. The shining sun produces the golden color of the tide. The reflection of the water becomes a symbol for *Shen* or spirit. The colorful wave becomes a symbol for the harmonization of fire and water. *Jing* is related to Metal, combining the *Yin* element of Water with the *Yang* element of the sun.

The journey of internal cultivation is not easy. In fact, it may be quite difficult, so it is necessary to continue to practice in order to purify the physical body and spiritual body, washing away resistance and blockages. The practice is not just about the movement, but about your inner world. You use the mind to purify all stagnations and wash away difficulties. The message becomes one of spiritual cultivation.

Movement: Bring your arms forward Raise your hands, with palm up, to chest level. Your hands are facing your chest. Inhale and bring your arms toward you; then exhale and let them flow out away from you. Repeat this movement a few times. It should be smooth and peaceful, mimicking the motion of ocean waves.

Visualization: Imagine a colorful wave in the sunlight washing and purifying your spirit. Feel the rhythmic motion of the tide as you merge yourself with this wave. Exhale and breathe out all negativity and toxins. Purify the deepest layer of your body.

Breathing: Inhale and bring your hands toward your body, then exhale as you turn your hands outward with the mantra *Hu*. (Your lips form a small hole and blow the air out).

Function: With this movement, we are washing the Heart and Lung, purifying our emotions. This movement promotes the structural, functional, and energetic wellness of the Heart and Lung. It also tonifies the spleen and aids in the release of the emotions belonging to the Heart, Lung and Spleen, namely anxiety and sadness. It works to purify the mind and *Shen* in general.

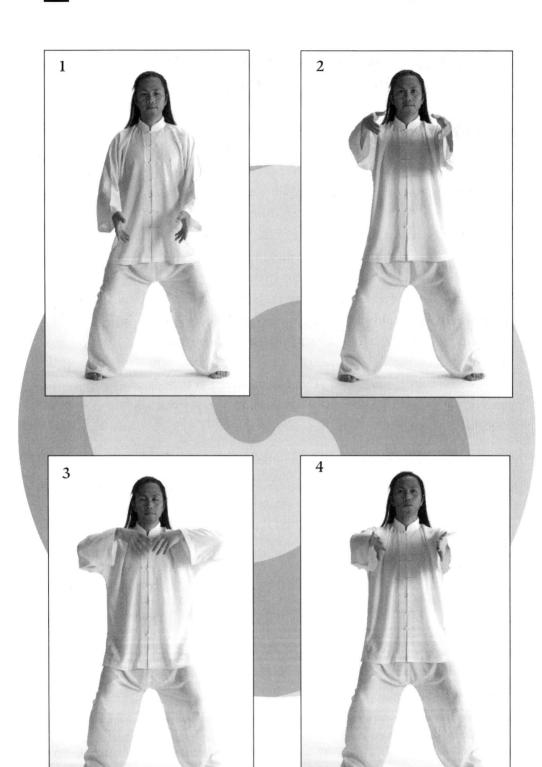

10.18 *Dan Feng Chao Yang* 丹鳳朝陽
—Red Phoenix Visits the Sun

Meaning: *Dan* means red, which is the color of spirit, and it also means elixir. *Feng* means phoenix, the symbol for the spirit. *Chao* means face but also means to meet someone in a higher position or from an older generation. Here, it means to raise your spiritual energy. *Yang* means the sun. The sun symbolizes the *Yang* energy of the universe and also the spirit of the body. In this movement, the Red Phoenix is the spiritual animal of the South and is therefore related to the Heart. The Red Phoenix visiting the sun represents the pure *Yang* state of cultivation, which refers to the body transforming into a state of immortality or Enlightenment. Through practicing this movement, we learn to purify our bodies and work through the difficulties involved in moving toward the pure *Yang* state and understanding the processes therein.

Movement: On the last exhale, breathe in again and bring your hands toward you. On your next exhale, snap your hands with palms forward and arms extended in front of you. Hold this circle as you raise your arms above your head and hold your posture.

Visualization: Imagine yourself as a Red Phoenix flying into Heaven and holding the sun up with your hands.

Breathing: Take a deep breath as you raise your arms over your head and hold your breath as long as you can. Exhale as your arms come down. Be mindful of lifting your perineum to hold onto the energy as you exhale.

Function: Holding this posture will strengthen your Fire and Earth energy since Fire gives birth to Earth. This movement strengthens the physical function of the shoulders and heart and also strengthens the spiritual function of the Heart *Shen* (spirit). It can assist in curing diarrhea.

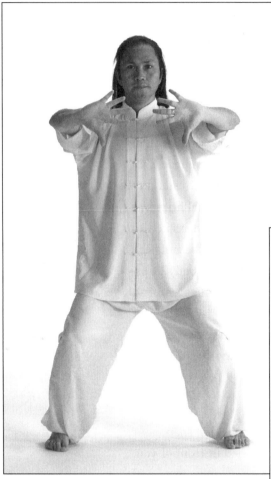

10.19 *Shui Zhong Lao Yue* 水中撈月 —Lift the Moon from the Water

Meaning: *Shui* means water. *Zhong* means center, within, or inside. *Lao* means pick up or lift. *Yue* means moon. The moon in the water is a symbol for emptiness. It is a symbol of the material world and the emptiness within it. The moon in the water is only a reflection of the physical moon that exists. *Qigong* practice can help us to deeply understand this emptiness. Everything in existence has some relationship, some connection, just as there is a moon in the water and there is a moon in the sky. Consequently, the reflection shows both emptiness and actual existence. The real emptiness is not emptiness because there is something there. There is an invisible universal law: We need to understand the Way in our cultivation. Once we dedicate ourselves to the Dao, we will learn the nature of emptiness and we can break our attachments to the material world. In a certain way, the material world brings resistance to our practice. Once we reach a high level of a pure *Yang* state and continue to move to higher and higher levels, it is still necessary to understand emptiness. Just as emptiness is infinite, our practice is infinite and should never stop, regardless of our level.

Movement: Inhale again, then exhale and begin to lower your arms and squat down. Draw a circle with your arms and hands, descending all the way down to the Earth while maintaining your posture with a straight back and neck. Keep the upper body straight, regardless of how low you go. When your arms and hands complete the circle, reach down to scoop up the moon from the bottom of the ocean. It is important to maintain the lift in your perineum and not let energy leak as you descend.

Visualization: Imagine pulling or lifting the moon out of the ocean.

Breathing: Lift your hands as you inhale deeply. Then hold your breath as long as you can. Remember to lift your perineum.

10.20 *Long Teng Hu Yue* 龍騰虎躍
—Dragon and Tiger Leap into Heaven

Meaning: *Long* means dragon. *Teng* means jumping or leaping. *Hu* means tiger. *Yue* means jump from one place to another, like jumping over a stream. *Yue* also means going to Heaven to connect with high-level beings. The leaping in this movement symbolizes two substances, *Qi* and *Jing*, which transform into *Shen*, and brings us closer to the Dao. This movement symbolizes East and West cooperating in *Yin-Yang* balance. In shamanism, the dragon and tiger are symbols for elevation. The dragon of the East represents *Yuanjing* 元精 or original essence in the body, while the tiger of the West represents *Yuanqi* 元气 or original *Qi*. These two substances combine and transform in the body to nourish *Shen*. Emptiness is not really emptiness in the literal sense. Emptiness symbolizes the universe that is woven together with *Qi* and is a vehicle for moving toward the Dao.

Movement: Pick up the moon and begin raising only your arms while still lifting your perineum and holding your posture. When your hands are at the level of your ears, rotate them with palms facing both sides and fingers pointing toward Heaven. Quickly jump up into Heaven and feel your fingers touching Heaven. Move your hips and stretch your arms upward.

Visualization: The left arm represents the dragon and the right arm represents the tiger. As these animals rise and leap into Heaven, feel your own fingers touching Heaven. Feel your whole body expanding.

Breathing: Hold your breath, and with a quick exhale, leap as you straighten your body. Your breath should be evenly regulated as you stretch with your two arms.

Function: This movement harmonizes the *Yin-Yang* energy. In the physical layer, it works to release any kind of disease. This movement transforms energy by opening the spiritual gates of the body and harmonizing the *Yin-Yang Qi* to purify the body. This allows for smooth energy flow and the unification of *Yin* and *Yang*. It is a way to refine the body's energy.

10.21 *Hui Feng Hun He* 迴風混合
—Harmonizing Wind Unites the Cosmos

Meaning: *Hui* means whirlpool and also means return. *Feng* means wind. In shamanism, *Feng* represents the circulation of *Qi*. *Hun* means blend, mix, or merge. *He* means combine, unite, union, harmony, or peace.

In *Qigong* practice, practitioners should always bring energy together to be refined in the "cauldron," which is located in the lower belly. One needs to control the wind very well to refine the energy. In Daoist internal alchemy, refining the elixir is a path to allow the mind, breath, and body to unite together in the last step to becoming symbolically immortal. After *Jing*, *Qi*, and *Shen* are harmonized and further refined, the practitioner will be enlightened and resonate with the Dao.

Movement: Rotate your fingers and wrists, holding the energy. Point your fingers toward Earth, bringing them to the level of your ears with your palms facing outward. Quickly lower your arms and legs with the *Heng* sound. Focus on your wrists and bring them down in a snapping motion with fingers pointing toward the waist. Remember your posture: head is upright, knees are bent in horse stance, and toes are grabbing the ground.

Visualization: Visualize all the light of the *Qi* condensing in your lower *Dantian*. Visualize and feel the *Dantian* as the center of the universe.

Breathing: The breath should be regulated to a softened state from the lower *Dantian*. Once you have moved into this state, the breath will become automatically regulated as you merge with the light and *Qi* in your lower *Dantian*.

Function: This movement enables us to move into a harmonizing *Qi* state so we can understand the Dao.

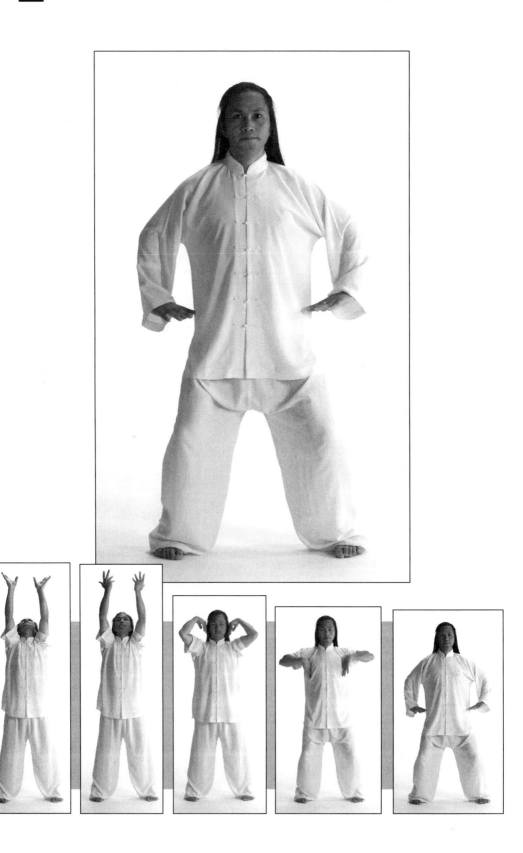

10.22 *Wei Ling Ba Fang* 威靈八方
—Maintain Peace in the Eight Directions

Meaning: *Wei* means dignity, power, or impressive presence. *Ling* is usually translated as soul, spirit, or shaman. *Ba* means eight and represents stableness and accomplishment. *Fang* means direction or way, and it stands for the cosmos. *Ba Fang* means eight directions, which includes all directions, the entire universe. You may start *Qigong* practice with a small personal request, such as to improve your state of health, to release life trauma, or to create the power to heal. After a certain period of *Qigong* practice, you will become aware that *Qigong* is a method for helping people live in a natural state. We need to learn how to reach this state by serving others rather than trying to fulfill personal desires.

This movement symbolizes bringing the benefits of immortality to the universe, not just to your personal world. It helps to deepen your power of compassion and to dedicate the practice and energy to others and to Mother Nature.

Movement: Keep holding your body posture (horse stance with your fingers pointing at your waist) as you move from side to side. Turn your head left as you shift to your left foot. Turn your head right as you shift to the right foot. Shift left and right a few times.

Visualization: Visualize driving off all evil energy, instilling and maintaining peace over the entire world.

Breathing: Exhale to either side as you imitate the roar of the tiger. Inhale when you switch sides and your head comes back to center.

Function: This movement strengthens the physical function of the whole body. It also increases healing power, especially the energy of compassion.

10.23 *Chao Li Dong Tian* 朝礼洞天 —Sacrifice Everything to the Heavenly Cave

Meaning: *Chao* means face or moving from a lower position to an upper position. *Li* means sacrifice, ritual, celebration, or humble. *Dong* means cave. *Tian* means Heaven or the universe. The connection is that human beings originated in a cave—a womb. In shamanic tradition, a cave is a sacred place in the body where your primordial spirit (*Yuanshen* 元神) dwells. It is also related to the tiger. The Queen Mother of the West lives in a cave, *Kunlunxu* 崑崙虚, which is covered with tiger skin. *Dong Tian* literally means Heavenly cave, and it is symbol of a special sacred place. Heavenly cave stands for the mystery of the Dao. This movement represents the concept that the human being is not separate from the universe. We need to remember the spiritual body and its universal root. In Chinese, we have a saying: "To give is the way to gain." In high-level *Qigong* cultivation, emptying your Heart and sacrificing yourself to the Dao is an important process. This is the secret of an enlightened being's ability to achieve immortality.

Movement: Stabilize your horse stance. Rotate your hands backward with palms up to extend behind you. Make a big circle with your arms coming forward and bring your feet together with your knees slightly bent and hold a prayerful attitude to rest in the *Taiji* mudra at the level of the middle *Dantian*. Males will place the left hand under the right, while females will place the right hand under the left. Your palms face Earth.

Visualization: Imagine gathering the Universal *Qi* when your feet and hands come together. Empty the physical body and the Heart-Mind. Dedicate the entirety of your being (mental, spiritual, and physical) to the Dao. You are returning to your cave.

Breathing: The breath is regulated from the lower *Dantian*. You can also perform holding-the-breath practice during this movement to further concentrate the energy in the lower *Dantian* and empty the Heart.

Function: This movement works to release the ego and desire, which is a pathway to access one's original nature. This movement may release any disease for self-healing. It is an especially good way to enhance the Heart and the spiritual energy. All disease is related to the Heart. As the Heart is sacrificed, the body will return to a natural state. In relation to this sacrifice, it is the shamanic tradition to always give your best to Heaven. When there is no giving, there is no gain. *Laozi* talked about this attitude of cultivation as *"Wai Qi Shen Er Shen Cun* 外其身而身存—The mind remains outside of the body, but the body is always there."[9] The actual meaning is: Take your body away from your mind and then your body will take care of itself.

10.24 *Dao Qi Chang Cun* 道炁常存
—Remain in the Dao *Qi*

Meaning: *Dao* means road, the Way, or universal law. As for the Great Dao itself, words cannot be used to interpret it, but you can experience it through your inner cultivation. *Qi* is the vital breath of the Dao, the universal life force. *Chang* means eternal, always, continue, or often. *Cun* means exist, be real, or live.

The Dao is omnipotent and omnipresent. It is everywhere all of the time. Through our practice, we can access the Dao anytime and anywhere. The Dao is not only for those who are enlightened beings; it is very close to ordinary human beings. We all have the ability to become enlightened. The difference is that the illuminated beings are living with the Dao, staying on the Path in their deepest consciousness, and regular people may be forgetting the Dao and living far away from it.

Movement: Lower your arms and release the *Taiji* mudra to return to the same posture as in the first movement. Make sure your posture is correct. Connect your *Laogong* with your lower *Dantian*. Be in the *Qi* field. Be in the Dao. Observe your inner landscape.

Visualization: Visualize being back in your cave. Imagine your whole being merging with the light of the Dao.

Breathing: Regulate your breath from the lower *Dantian*. Soften your breath to a slow, smooth, deep, and even state.

Function: This movement maintains physical well being and awakens within us the eternal Dao which is always present. Actually, this movement looks like doing nothing but it is an important part of *Qigong* practice. We need to move into the state of tranquility to cultivate our inner knowledge after all active movements. This is a way to experience the Dao. This is the essence of *Qigong* passed on by ancient Chinese shamans to help people learn the eternal Dao. *Laozi* states this process in his *Daodejing* as: "The sages (shamans) conduct their business with actionless actions and give their teachings with wordless words."[10]

Afterword

In September 2005, after I had finished the final draft of this book, I had a great experience of nature in Hawaii with my wife Deirdre Orceyre. I practiced my shamanic alchemy *Qigong* on the *Kan* 坎 (Water) island of Kauai and the *Li* 離 (Fire) island of the Big Island. I sensed the power of Water and Fire and how they destroy and recreate life. The abundance of nature that is so evident in Hawaii showed me the importance of the symbolic "killing" function of the tiger. Death is indeed the path of rebirth. Through the gifts from my students and friends Malik Cotter and Joyanna Cotter, I had the chance to visit the House of the Sun, Haleakala, and the Valley of the Moon, Iao, on the island of Maui. I thought about the topic of Enlightenment as I was enjoying the magic of Maui and meditating in the bright light of the sun and the moon.

When I returned to my home in Portland, Oregon, I received Dr. Lonny Jarrett's insightful commentary on my book. One of the interesting and important ideas he wrote to me about was Enlightenment. He suggested I go into more depth on the topic of Enlightenment at the end of this book. To do this, I felt that I needed a quiet space with a cup of tea to write about this in an afterword to conclude this book. I am now in the woods enjoying the natural breeze, meditating in the green and golden colors of the forest, listening to the singing of the birds, drinking the tea, and continuing my writing. My thanks to David Branscomb and his wife Laura Hauer for their generous offering of this space for my personal retreat and writing.

Now let us drink tea and join Dr. Jarrett in his discussion: "What is Enlightenment? Since this is the path and the goal, a discussion of Enlightenment seems to be in order. The *Wu* (ancient shamans) were connected to the unborn, the simplicity on the infantile side of complexity. It seems to me that Enlightenment is the simplicity on the other side of complexity." Dr. Jarrett wrote the Chinese character *Ming* 明 for Enlightenment in his discussion.

So then, what is Enlightenment? We use this word almost every day in our *Qigong* practice and in other spiritual cultivation practices. Let us begin with the meaning of the Chinese character *Ming* 明 for Enlightenment. *Ming* 明 is composed of the left radical *Ri* 日 for the sun and the right radical *Yue* 月 for the moon. As we learned in Part I, 3 *Dong Xi Yuan Tong*—The Pathway of *Yin Yang*, a traditional way to learn the *Dao* 道 is to observe the sun and the moon. Therefore, the original meaning of *Ming* is "understand the Dao." More common meanings of *Ming* are bright, clear, understand, brilliant, and pure-hearted. Through studying the meanings of *Ming*, we may learn about the different degrees of spiritual Enlightenment. The sun and moon are symbols that fully represent brightness. We can see things clearly when the light breaks down the darkness, and we can see better when more light is available to us.

Consciousness is the light of the Heart. We are able to understand more about the truth of our lives as we awaken more of our consciousness. The degree of the awakening of consciousness is the degree of spiritual Enlightenment. The full awakening of consciousness is full Enlightenment. A fully enlightened being lives with the prenatal, eternal, or original Heart (*Benxing* 本性). With this Eternal Heart, the enlightened being understands the Dao and lives with the Dao in every moment. We call this being Immortal or Buddha.

At the most common level, Enlightenment carries only the common meaning of *Ming*—understand. I want to share another common Chinese word for understand, *Zhidao* 知道, which is literally translated as "understand the Dao." Most Chinese people casually say, "*Wo Zhidao*"—"I understand the Dao," but they do not really understand the Dao. Let us have some tea and continue this discussion.

Tea is tea, before Enlightenment. Do you remember the first time we drank tea? Yes, we did not know how to drink the tea, and we could not tell the differences in quality. No matter the kind, they were all just tea. This is equal to the beginning of our *Qigong* practice or other spiritual cultivation practices. We can't tell the differences among all the practice forms.

Tea is not tea, during Enlightenment. After we learned how to drink the tea and spent a lot of time drinking different kinds of tea, we were excited to tell our friends how much we "understand" tea. Do we really understand tea? This

is the normal level of Enlightenment. Similarly, after we learn how to practice *Qigong*, we say, "I know *Qigong*." Do we really "know" *Qigong*?

Tea is tea, after Enlightenment. The style of a tea master drinking tea may be no different from that of a beginner. Tea masters drink the tea without excitement or criticism. Tea is tea; the tea masters enjoy it and live with it. This is the highest Enlightenment. We may not be able to tell that they are enlightened beings when we meet them because they might appear to be living an ordinary lifestyle.

Now let us imagine we are having a tea party. Two new guests join us, a tea master and a beginning tea drinker. Both of them lift their teacups and drink their tea without any words. Can you tell who is who? What is the difference between a fully enlightened being and an ordinary person? A Chinese proverb says, "*Da Zhi Rou Yu* 大智若愚 "—A person with great wisdom may look like a foolish person. These discussions are related to Dr. Jarrett's other thoughts: "To what degree is spiritual Enlightenment correlated with physical health? Ramana Maharshi, a great and fully enlightened being, died of cancer." Yes, in my understanding, a fully enlightened being should not have physical health problems. Why did some of those enlightened beings die from physical illnesses? I want to leave these discussions for my next book, *The Way of Enlightenment— Chinese Shamanic 28 Lunar Mansions Cosmic Qigong*. Also, I believe that you will have your answers to these questions when you drink more tea.

At this moment, I can hear the calls of the wild geese flying over my roof. As I lift my head and look at the sky through the window, I see that a group of geese is forming the shape of the Chinese character *Ren* 人 (person) toward the south. Oh, it reminds me that it is autumn— the tiger season. Moreover, it inspires many thoughts. Why did the ancient *Wu* 巫 regard the wild goose as a symbol for spiritual Enlightenment? Do the geese understand the Dao? Yes. Of course, yes! Why did the *Wu* 巫 use the shape of migrating geese as the character to represent the human being? This character is so simple; it is made with only two strokes— one left and one right. Oh yes, the left and right is the pathway of *Yin* and *Yang*. *Ren* is a pattern of the Dao. The Dao is within us. We are all enlightened beings on the path to becoming fully enlightened!

The great Dao is very simple and very close to us. The Dao is within the tea. Enlightenment is within the tea. Let us *Pin* 品 (savor) it.

Zhongxian Wu

Hermitage Cottage, Cloud Mountain Retreat Center

October 16, 2005

Footnotes Part I

1. Laozi. *Daodejing*. Chapter 35.

2. Laozi. *Daodejing*. Chapter 12.

3. *Yijing*. *Xici* (Appended Statements). See *Zhouyi Shangshixue*. Beijing: Zhonghua Shuju. 1988: 304. There are ten commentaries to the *Yijing*. It is commonly believed that Confucius wrote them to assist modern people in understanding the terse and cryptic language of the original text. Today these are included with the *Yijing* and are referred to as the "Ten Wings" because they assist our minds in understanding the deeper meanings and thus help us achieve greater heights. *Xici* is one of the Ten Wings.

4. *Dantian* literally means elixir field. It is located in the lower belly. Its function is the storage of the life force.

5. Wu, Zhongxian. "Dancing and Drumming – Feeling the 'Rhythm' of Qigong, Calligraphy, and *Wu* (Shamanism)." Empty Vessel Fall 2003: 36.

6. Liu, An. *Huainanzi*. Chapter 8.

7. Confucius. *Lun Yu* (The Analects). Chapter 7.

8. Shima, Qian. *Shiji: Zhuan* (Biography.) *Siku Quanshu* (Four Reservoirs of Ancient Texts) 1773.

9. Wu, Zhongxian. "The Cauldron and the Horse: Internal Cultivation and *Yijing*." Taijiquan Journal Summer 2003: 14.

10. This sentence appears in Hexagram 44 (*Gou*) in the *Yijing*. It occurs in Chapter 66 of the *Huangdi Neijing* as well.

11. Laozi. *Daodejing*. Chapter 73.

12. Laozi. *Daodejing*. Chapter 25.

13. *Huangdi Neijing*. Chapter 5 of Suwen.

14. Wu, Zhongxian. "Internal Cultivation and *Yijing*." Taijiquan Journal Summer 2003: 17.

15. *Huangdi Neijing*. Chapter 5 of Suwen.

16. Wu, Zhongxian. "Internal Cultivation and *Yijing*." Taijiquan Journal Summer 2003: 14.

Footnotes Part II

1. Laozi, *Daodejing*, Chapter 42.

2. Wu, Zhongxian. "The Cauldron and the Horse: Internal Cultivation and *Yijing*." <u>Taijiquan Journal</u> Summer 2003: 12-17.

3. Yuan, Ke. *Shanhaijing Jiaozhu*. Chengdu: Bashu Shushe. 1996: 466.

4. Yuan, Ke. *Shanhaijing Jiaozhu*. Chengdu: Bashu Shushe. 1996: 59.

5. Yuan, Ke. *Shanhaijing Jiaozhu*. Chengdu: Bashu Shushe. 1996: 357 – 358.

6. *The Great Dictionary of Chinese Religions and Mythology*. Beijing: XueYuan ChuBanShe. 1990: 265.

7. Li, Shizhen. *Bencao Gangmu*.

8. See *Fengsu Tongyi*.

9. Normally, people think *"Wu* 无 *"* is the simplified character of *"Wu* 無 *"* and prefer to write "无極" as " 無極 " Actually, "无 " is the original character in " 无極" and it is related with the character *Tian* 天 for Heaven.

10. Laozi, *Daodejing*, Chapter 25.

11. This Chu State *Bamboo Book* was discovered in the Chu State tomb (340-320 BCE) at Guodian, in Jingmen, Hubei, China in 1993. It was reprinted in 1998. *Guodian Chumu Zhujian*. Beijing: Wenwu Chubanshe, 1998: 194.

12. *Yijing*, Xici.

13. Quoted in Wu, Zhongxian. "The Cauldron and the Horse: Internal Cultivation And *Yijing*." <u>Taijiquan Journal</u>, Summer 2003: 14.

14. Liu, An. *Hauinanzi* 淮南子. Chapter 7, *Lanminxun* 覽冥訓.

15. See Wu, Zhongxian. "Seeking the Roots of Classical *Qigong*: Exploring the Original Meaning of the Pure Yang Mudra." <u>Empty Vessel</u> Winter 2003: 26.

16. Li, Jingde. *Zhuzi yulei*, comp. (1270; rpt Beijing: Zhonghua shuju, 1986), 3:37.

17. Translated by Louis Komjathy. Inward Training. Seattle: Wandering Cloud Press 2003: 3.

18. Wu, Zhongxian. *Qigong Yu Renshen (Qigong and Your Life)*. Shaanxi Luyou Chubanshe: Xian, P.R.of China.1996: 40-44.

19. Zhang, Sanfeng. *Dazhuoge (Meditation Mantra)*. Reprinted in Complete Collections of *Zhang Sanfeng*. Hangzou:Zhejiang Guji Chubanshe.1999:29.

20. Ibid.

21. Laozi, *Daodejing*, Chapter 21.

22. Chang, *K.C. Art, Myth, and Ritual: The Path to Political Authority in Ancient China*. Cambridge: Harvard University Press. 1983: 45-47.

23. See Wu, Zhongxian, "Dancing and Drumming – Feeling the 'Rhythm' of *Qigong*, Calligraphy, and Wu (Shamanism)." <u>Qi-Journal</u> Winter 2003-2004: 25.

24. Karcher, Stephen. *Ta Chuan*. New York: St. Martin's Press. 2000: 40.

25. Li, Zehou, *Jimao Wu Shuo*. Beijing: Zhongguo Dianying Chubanshe, 1999: 68.

26. See Footnotes Part I , 3.

27. Chen, Lai, *Gudai Zongjiao yu Lunli—Lujia Shixiang de Geyuan*. Beijing: Sanlian Shudian, 1996: 35.

28. Zhang, Jiebing. "*Yi yi yi*" in *Leijing Fuyi* (Ming Dynasty) reprinted in Xian: Shaanxi Kexue Jishu Chubanshe. 1996: 350.

29. Liu, An. *Huananzi*, Chapter 1.

30. Liu, Xiaolu. *Zhongguo Bohua*. Shanghai: Shanghai Guji Chubanshe. 1994. 26.

31. In Chinese mythology, there were ten suns in ancient times.

32. Bajaj, Kipp R. The *Wu*: Early Chinese Adepts in the Art of Transforming Matter and Spirit. Masters thesis for M.S. in Oriental Medicine 2003: 23.

33. Wu, Zhongxian. "The Cauldron and the Horse: Internal Cultivation and *Yijing*." <u>Taijiquan Journal</u> 2003: 12-17.

34. Laozi. *Daodejing*. Chapter 60.

35. For details see Wu, Zhongxian, "The Cauldron and the Horse: Internal Cultivation and *Yijing*." <u>Taijiquan Journal</u> 2003:12-17.

Footnotes Part III

1. Laozi. *Daodejing*. Chapter 1.

2. This citation is from *Tang* Dynasty (617-907 AC) famous scholar Hanyu's *Shishou*.

3. Redfield, Robert. Peasant Society and Culture. Chicago: The University of Chicago Press. 1960: 41-45.

4. Li, Zehou. *Jimao Wushuo*. Beijing: Zhongguo Dianying Chubanshe. 1999: 65-66.

5. Zhang, Jiebing. "Yi yi yi." *Leijing Fuyi*. Xian: Shaanxi Kexue Jishu Chubanshe. 1996: 350.

6. Chen, Lai. *Gudai Zongjiao yu Lunli - Lujia Shixiang de Geyuan*. Beijing: Sanlian Shudian. 1996: 35.

7. Wu, Zhongxian. "Dancing and Drumming – Feeling the 'Rhythm' of *Qigong*, Calligraphy, and *Wu* (Shamanism)." Qi-Journal Winter 2003-2004.

8. Confucius. *Xici*, one of the Ten Wings of *Yijing*.

9. Laozi. *Daodejing*. Chapter 7.

10. Laozi. *Daodejing*. Chapter 2.

About the Author

Master **Zhongxian Wu** was born on China's eastern shore in the city of *Wenling* in *Zhejiang* Province, where the sun's rays first touch the Chinese mainland. He began practicing *Qigong*, calligraphy, and *Taiji* at an early age. Inspired by the immediate strengthening effects of this practice, Master Wu committed himself to the life-long pursuit of the ancient arts of internal cultivation. He devoted himself to the study of *Qigong*, martial arts, Chinese medicine, *Yijing* science, Chinese calligraphy, and ancient Chinese music over the next thirty years, studying with some of the best teachers in these fields.

Master Wu is the lineage holder of four different schools of *Qigong* and martial arts:

- 18th generation lineage holder of the Mt. Wudang Dragon Gate style of *Qigong* (*Wudang Longmen Pai*)

- 8th generation lineage holder of the Mt. Emei Sage/Shaman style *Qigong* (*Emei Zhengong*)

- 7th generation lineage holder of the Dai Family Heart Method style of *Xin Yi* (*Dai Shi Xinyi Quan*)

- 12th generation lineage holder of the Wudang He style of *Taijiquan*.

In China, Master Wu served as Director of the *Shaanxi* Province Association for Somatic Science and the *Shaanxi* Association for the Research of Daoist Nourishing Life Practices. In this capacity, he conducted many investigations into the clinical efficacy of *Qigong* and authored five books and numerous articles on the philosophical and historical foundations of China's ancient life sciences. Since he began teaching in 1988, Master Wu has instructed thousands of *Qigong* students, Eastern and Western.

In 2001, Master Wu left his job as an engineer in *Xi'an,* China, to come to the United States to teach *Qigong.* For four years he served as Senior Instructor and Resident Expert of *Qigong* and *Taiji* in the Classical Chinese Medicine Department at the National College of Naturopathic Medicine (NCNM) in Portland, Oregon. In addition to his work at NCNM, Master Wu was a sub-investigator in a 2003 *Qigong* research program sponsored by the U.S. National Institutes of Health (NIH). Currently, Master Wu presents trainings and workshops for professionals and the general public in *Qigong* and *Taiji* and on topics related to the classical Chinese arts. ***Vital Breath of the Dao—Chinese Shamanic Tiger Qigong (Laohu Gong 老虎功)*** is Master Wu's first *Qigong* book in English.

Master Wu is committed to bringing the authentic teachings of Chinese ancient wisdom tradition such as *Qigong, Taiji,* martial arts, calligraphy, Chinese astrology, and *Yijing* science to his students. In addition to his classes, workshops, and seminars, he offers a long-term *Qigong* and *Taiji* training program that provides a strong foundation for the study of shamanic *Qigong,* internal alchemy, *Taiji* and *Qi*-healing skills, including classical Chinese energy techniques, medical *Qigong,* and martial arts applications.

To contact Master Wu visit www.masterwu.net

Index

Strengthen Your Immune System, Enhance Your Flexibility, Heal More Effectively and Achieve Deep Inner Peace—With The Ancient Power of *Chinese Shamanic Tiger Qigong*

Chinese Shamanic Tiger Qigong is a uniquely potent practice designed to bolster our health and deepen our spiritual connection to universal energy. Lineage holder, **Master Zhongxian Wu** provides detailed instruction in this powerful *Mt. Emei Sage Style* 24-movement Qigong form, which combines the traditions of ancient shamanism, Confucianism, Daoism, classical Chinese medicine, and the martial arts.

The tiger is a symbol for shamanic power and for Qi, especially *Zhengqi*. Physically, *Zhengqi* is represented most strongly by the Lung, which prevents pathogenic Qi from invading the body. The Lung governs and energizes all the meridians of the body, helping us to achieve and maintain a high level of resilient well being.

- **Awakens** energy and consciousness in your body—to feel more alive and more grounded
- **Develops** your shamanic healing abilities—to effectively alleviate others' suffering
- **Opens** your energy gates and meridians—to achieve long lasting, buoyant health
- **Strengthens** your immune system—to better protect you from disease
- **Allows** the free flow of Qi—to connect with universal energy and attain deep levels of tranquility

- **Connects** you to nature's deepest healing powers—to rebound more strongly from past health challenges
- **Enhances** your flexibility and mobility—to enjoy easier, pain-free movement
- **Relaxes** your body and mind—to reduce unwanted tension and stress

Chinese Shamanic Tiger Qigong
Laohu Gong
With Master Zhongxian Wu

DVD
Running time: 65 minutes

#DV031 $39.95

Receive our FREE magazine *VITALICS* and visit our website www.dragondoor.com—to boost your qigong knowledge and skill

Discover a wealth of articles, blogs and other resources to keep you current with the best in qigong and related health resources.

Call Dragon Door Publications at 1-800-899-5111 to request your FREE VITALICS catalog, or order it from our website, www.dragondoor.com

ORDERING INFORMATION

Customer Service Questions? Please call us between 9:00am– 11:00pm EST Monday to Friday at 1-800-899-5111. Local and foreign customers call 513-346-4160 for orders and customer service

100% One-Year Risk-Free Guarantee. If you are not completely satisfied with any product–for any reason, no matter how long after you received it–we'll be happy to give you a prompt exchange, credit, or refund, as you wish. Simply return your purchase to us, and please let us know why you were dissatisfied–it will help us to provide better products and services in the future. *Shipping and handling fees are non-refundable.*

Telephone Orders For faster service you may place your orders by calling Toll Free 24 hours a day, 7 days a week, 365 days per year. When you call, please have your credit card ready.

1·800·899·5111
24 HOURS A DAY
FAX YOUR ORDER (866) 280-7619

Complete and mail with full payment to: Dragon Door Publications, P.O. Box 1097, West Chester, OH 45071

Please print clearly

Sold To: A
Name_____
Street_____
City_____
State _____ Zip _____
Day phone*_____
*Important for clarifying questions on orders

Please print clearly

SHIP TO: *(Street address for delivery)*   B
Name_____
Street_____
City_____
State _____ Zip _____
Email_____

Warning to foreign customers:
The Customs in your country may or may not tax or otherwise charge you an additional fee for goods you receive. Dragon Door Publications is charging you only for U.S. handling and international shipping. Dragon Door Publications is in no way responsible for any additional fees levied by Customs, the carrier or any other entity.

Item #	Qty.	Item Description	Item Price	A or B	Total

HANDLING AND SHIPPING CHARGES · NO COD'S

Total Amount of Order Add:

Total Amount of Order	Add		Total Amount of Order	Add
$00.00 to $24.99	add $5.00		$100.00 to $129.99	add $12.00
$25.00 to $39.99	add $6.00		$130.00 to $169.99	add $14.00
$40.00 to $59.99	add $7.00		$170.00 to $199.99	add $16.00
$60.00 to $99.99	add $10.00		$200.00 to $299.99	add $18.00
			$300.00 and up	add $20.00

Canada & Mexico add $8.00. All other countries triple U.S. charges.

Total of Goods	
Shipping Charges	
Rush Charges	
Kettlebell Shipping Charges	
OH residents add 6% sales tax	
MN residents add 6.5% sales tax	
Total Enclosed	

Method of Payment ___Check ___M.O. ___Mastercard ___Visa ___Discover ___Amex
Account No. *(Please indicate all the numbers on your credit card)*   EXPIRATION DATE

☐☐☐☐ ☐☐☐☐ ☐☐☐☐ ☐☐☐☐   ☐☐/☐☐
Day Phone (   )
_____

SIGNATURE_____   DATE _____

NOTE: We ship best method available for your delivery address. Foreign orders are sent by air. Credit card or International M.O. only. For rush processing of your order, add an additional $10.00 per address. Available on money order & charge card orders only.

Errors and omissions excepted. Prices subject to change without notice.

ORDERING INFORMATION

Customer Service Questions? Please call us between 9:00am– 11:00pm EST Monday to Friday at 1-800-899-5111. Local and foreign customers call 513-346-4160 for orders and customer service

100% One-Year Risk-Free Guarantee. If you are not completely satisfied with any product–for any reason, no matter how long after you received it–we'll be happy to give you a prompt exchange, credit, or refund, as you wish. Simply return your purchase to us, and please let us know why you were dissatisfied–it will help us to provide better products and services in the future. *Shipping and handling fees are non-refundable.*

Telephone Orders For faster service you may place your orders by calling Toll Free 24 hours a day, 7 days a week, 365 days per year. When you call, please have your credit card ready.

1·800·899·5111
24 HOURS A DAY
FAX YOUR ORDER (866) 280-7619

Complete and mail with full payment to: Dragon Door Publications, P.O. Box 1097, West Chester, OH 45071

Please print clearly

Sold To: A

Name_____

Street_____

City_____

State_____ Zip_____

Day phone*_____
*Important for clarifying questions on orders

Please print clearly

SHIP TO: *(Street address for delivery)* B

Name_____

Street_____

City_____

State_____ Zip_____

Email_____

Warning to foreign customers:
The Customs in your country may or may not tax or otherwise charge you an additional fee for goods you receive. Dragon Door Publications is charging you only for U.S. handling and international shipping. Dragon Door Publications is in no way responsible for any additional fees levied by Customs, the carrier or any other entity.

Item #	Qty.	Item Description	Item Price	A or B	Total

HANDLING AND SHIPPING CHARGES • NO COD'S

Total Amount of Order Add:

$00.00 to $24.99 add $5.00	$100.00 to $129.99 add $12.00
$25.00 to $39.99 add $6.00	$130.00 to $169.99 add $14.00
$40.00 to $59.99 add $7.00	$170.00 to $199.99 add $16.00
$60.00 to $99.99 add $10.00	$200.00 to $299.99 add $18.00
	$300.00 and up add $20.00

Canada & Mexico add $8.00. All other countries triple U.S. charges.

Total of Goods	
Shipping Charges	
Rush Charges	
Kettlebell Shipping Charges	
OH residents add 6% sales tax	
MN residents add 6.5% sales tax	
Total Enclosed	

METHOD OF PAYMENT ___CHECK ___M.O. ___MASTERCARD ___VISA ___DISCOVER ___AMEX

Account No. *(Please indicate all the numbers on your credit card)*   EXPIRATION DATE

☐☐☐☐ ☐☐☐☐ ☐☐☐☐ ☐☐☐☐   ☐☐/☐☐

Day Phone (   )

_____

SIGNATURE_____ DATE _____

NOTE: We ship best method available for your delivery address. Foreign orders are sent by air. Credit card or International M.O. only. For rush processing of your order, add an additional $10.00 per address. Available on money order & charge card orders only.

Errors and omissions excepted. Prices subject to change without notice.

DDP 01/05